OTHER TITLES OF INTEREST FROM ST. LUCIE PRESS

The 90-Day ISO 9000 Manual and Implementation Guide

The Executive Guide to Implementing Quality Systems

Focused Quality: Managing for Results

Improving Service Quality: Achieving High Performance in the Public and
   Private Sectors

Introduction to Modern Statistical Quality Control and Management

ISO 9000: Implementation Guide for Small to Mid-Sized Businesses

Organization Teams: Continuous Quality Improvement

Organization Teams: Facilitator's Guide

Principles of Total Quality

Quality Improvement Handbook: Team Guide to Tools and Techniques

The Textbook of Total Quality in Healthcare

Total Quality in Higher Education

Total Quality in Managing Human Resources

Total Quality in Marketing

Total Quality in Purchasing and Supplier Management

Total Quality in Radiology: A Guide to Implementation

Total Quality in Research and Development

Total Quality Management for Custodial Operations

Total Quality Management: Text, Cases, and Readings, 2nd Edition

Total Quality Service

For more information about these titles call, fax or write:

St. Lucie Press
100 E. Linton Blvd., Suite 403B
Delray Beach, FL 33483
TEL (407) 274-9906 • FAX (407) 274-9927

S^t_L

Mastering the Diversity Challenge

Easy on-the-job applications for measurable results

Mastering the Diversity Challenge

*Easy on-the-job applications
for measurable results*

Fern Lebo

S_L^t

St. Lucie Press
Delray Beach, Florida

Printed and bound in the U.S.A. Printed on acid-free paper.
10 9 8 7 6 5 4 3 2 1

ISBN 1-884015-35-2

Direct all inquiries to St. Lucie Press, Inc., 100 E. Linton Blvd., Suite 403B, Delray Beach, Florida 33483.

Phone: (407) 274-9906
Fax: (407) 274-9927

AJJ7322

S^{t}L

Published by
St. Lucie Press
100 E. Linton Blvd., Suite 403B
Delray Beach, FL 33483

CONTENTS

PREFACE

"The forces of homogenized culture are already in full retreat." At least that's what NBC's popular news magazine program "Sunday Morning" reported in March 1993. Well, maybe. Diversity seminars, workshops, lectures and courses, currently in vogue across the continent, are certainly indicators of an increased sensitivity to a changing work force. Indeed, the fact that you are reading this book points to your own expanded awareness or perhaps to your concern. What with mandates, legislation, affirmative action and protected classes, you probably realize that you will have to interfere with knee-jerk reactions to a changing environment to improve the likelihood of your own success. But here's the kicker. While diversity management has become a hot new topic, it has also taken on an interesting twist: how to help the disadvantaged or different to "fit in," which may, in itself, may be counterproductive to your management goals.

The upsurge in diversity awareness may indicate some nice little baby steps in the right direction, but when the talk turns to helping "the others" to fit the mold, as it so often does, it is clear that there is a big job ahead. It is also immediately obvious that a lot of people just don't get it. And they are usually the ones in positions of power.

Defining Diversity Issues

The future ain't what it used to be.

Yogi Berra

It used to be that you did your job, followed the rules and looked forward to a long and stable future with your organization. It used to be that you took charge, modeled yourself after your boss, demonstrated loyalty and a "nose to the grindstone" attitude, and could count on a work force that fell in line. It used to be that when you were hired as a supervisor or manager, you could call the shots, interpret differences as deficiencies, fear no reprisals and maybe even expect some reward. That's what used to be.

In today's world of organizational renewal, restructuring, reorganization and retrenchment, what used to be just isn't anymore. In today's rapidly changing marketplace, organizations need something more from all their employees. And that means they need something more from you.

Traditionally, we Americans have quietly prided ourselves on our stoic acceptance of the great "melting pot" theory, on being tolerant and broad-minded. While we were quick to brag about multi-culturalism, we simultaneously focused on the assimilation of newcomers and boasted about our willingness to embrace outsiders and turn them into real citizens. But valuing diversity means being and doing none of those things. To value differences, I as an individual must understand, at the deepest level, that people who look, think or behave differently from me are not likely to want to copy me or to be me. They are exactly who they are. They want to be neither tolerated nor merely accepted by others who profess to be broad-minded. They do want to be respected and valued, not in spite of their differences but, perhaps, even because of them.

In his ground-breaking book *Beyond Race and Gender*, Dr. R Roosevelt Thomas, Jr. helps to clarify the issues, beginning with a comparative analysis of current "diversity" terminology. He first explains affirmative action or employment equity initiatives as "special efforts" in the creation of a diverse work force. These efforts are generally legally required and compliance driven. They take the form of such measures as actively promoting minority members or hiring specific numbers of targeted groups to ensure that a particular work force reflects the community in which it finds itself. Thomas then describes valuing diversity as "understanding, respecting and valuing differences among various groups." Seminars and workshops on valuing diversity often take the form of sensitivity-raising sessions or cross-cultural experiences, promoted in an effort to improve interpersonal relationships among members of a diverse work force. Lastly, Thomas characterizes managing diversity as "creating an environment appropriate for full utilization of a diverse work force." This is a management matter with a focus on gaining a business advantage in a competitive marketplace. And that's what this book is all about.

In practical terms, affirmative action is usually a numbers game in response to legal requirements, and if you simply want to satisfy affirmative action regulations, you will be out of luck in your efforts toward creating a culture that values differences. Valuing diversity means cherishing and capitalizing on differences because it is those very differences that add value and enrich our lives, our organizations and our country, offering variety, originality and an untapped source of human capital. *Managing diversity is a business management issue.* It means managing a diverse work force with the same primary goal once advocated when a homogeneous work force was the norm: maximum individual development and opportunity for maximum individual growth and productivity. That goal is valid today and is one that benefits both the individual and the company.

When an organization decides to institute "valuing diversity" policies and programs, because of either internal or external pressure to do so, or in response to a well-meaning sense of moral imperative, the first step is to help that organization define what valuing diversity means, because whatever it means, it promises change. As some clever guru once noted, while change is not the enemy, uncertainty is. Any culture change can be a treacherous adversary because it is a shadowy process; nobody knows for sure what the change will do to them personally, and it scares them. Uncertainty about one's future can be terrifying. To conquer the fear, an organization must target the human element.

In *Surviving Corporate Transition*, William Bridges, Ph.D., explains the difficulty with change. Even when everyone involved recognizes that the mandated change is good and necessary, the change itself creates a powerful sense of loss for what used to be. Letting go of the past is difficult, no matter how distasteful, unfair or uncomfortable that past may have been. Change creates resistance, says Bridges; the bigger the change, the greater the resistance. To minimize resistance to change, and to ensure that everyone is on board, you must anticipate the human response to change and begin the process of managing for change.

If your company is only concerned about covering itself legally, your job will be relatively easy. Access to guidelines on legal requirements is readily available from any number of experts who will, in a brief session, outline the legal issues, including hiring practices, equity questions, work environment requirements, harassment policies, systemic barriers and wrongful dismissal concerns. These experts will advise whether or not a company may legally ask a prospective employee, in a pre-employment interview, about the derivation of their unusual name, where they were born, if they have any handicaps or (of women) how many children they plan to have. (These questions may not be asked.)

If, however, your company plans to tackle diversity on a deeper, human level, your task will be bigger. A poor but common place to start is by hiring or promoting unqualified people. It sets them up for defeat and gives others reason to whisper "I told you so."

A good place to start, indeed the only sensible place to start, is to get a picture of where you are now so you know how far you have to go.

There are a variety of ways to get that picture, several of which are addressed in Chapter 2: Creating the Motivational Climate. Once you have a handle on where you are, you will want some specific ideas on where to go from there. This book has a broad array of checklists, suggestions, ideas and approaches to help you make the changes you want, to help you manage your diverse work force. There is space for you to include your own thoughts, lists to get you started on generating ideas of your own and exercises designed to get everyone involved.

Like any good handbook, you don't have to read it from cover to cover. *Mastering the Diversity Challenge* has been carefully designed for easy access to precisely the information you need—to be used exactly when you need it. This book will give you a variety of tools and strategies for:

- Improving your general management skills

- Breaking through obstacles to peak performance

- Improving communication

- Enhancing your probability of success by creating a climate that encourages the success of everyone for whom you are responsible

- Improving initiative in areas of accountability

- Making all your staff an asset to the organization by helping them achieve their performance potential

- Motivating your staff to make a significant contribution

- Building awareness and support for diversity initiatives at every level of the organization.

In a step-by-step, easy-to-use format, this book explains why there is a good business case for managing diversity. It identifies issues specific to the designated groups and others and provides effective techniques for creating a level playing field. Perhaps most importantly, it addresses specific on-the-job applications. You know you can do it; it just takes time and effort. Remember, genius is perseverance in disguise. Simply pick out the pieces you want, and enjoy the credit for managing to make a real difference.

As you flip through the pages, you will see a number of tests, questionnaires, games, stories and ideas. Their use is limited only by your imagination. You are the manager; you can choose any one you like and use it:

- As an ice breaker to open meetings
- As a discussion topic to build the team
- To open the dialogue for one-on-one meetings
- As homework to increase sensitivity
- For coaching and counseling
- To educate and "grow" your people
- As a strategy for improving communication
- As a way to convey "I care what we're all about"

Thanks

Special thanks to Bram Lebo, LL.B., M.B.A., M.B.I., for his support and assistance in the preparation of this book. Thanks are also due to Lewis Eisen, LL.B., whose insights and editing skills were invaluable.

AUTHOR

Fern Lebo is President of Lebo Communications, an innovative company providing consultation and training in support of diversity management initiatives. As a change management consultant, she designs and presents diversity training seminars targeted to meet the needs of her corporate clients.

Her training as a psychotherapist specializing in group dynamics brings a professional's insights and approach to the materials she develops. Early in her career, she was a clinical therapist and tutorial leader and worked in association with three major Canadian universities. Currently, her expertise in human issues has made her an invaluable resource in the corporate arena.

Fern draws the best out of her students by challenging them to break away from their comfort zones of familiar but often non-constructive behavior patterns. She partners with a broad variety of public and private sector clients and creates customized results-driven programs to support new directions. Her focus is on enabling every employee to achieve peak performance within the context of a diverse work force targeting organizational goals.

An internationally published author, Fern has written several books and innumerable articles and is a regular contributor to professional and trade journals. She has also been a frequent guest on Canadian and American radio and television talk shows and is a regular speaker at international training conferences and meetings.

THE DIVERSITY ISSUE IN MANAGEMENT TODAY

1

Even if you have not been specifically charged with the responsibility of managing diversity, as a manager, supervisor or leader, you have to do it. Even if everyone in your jurisdiction looks a lot like they could actually be cousins, the fact is that they are a group of individuals, each with his or her own unique talents, skills, strengths and weaknesses. They are diverse. And as a manager, supervisor or leader, you want this diverse group of people to consistently deliver because, to paraphrase a well-known commercial, if they don't look good, you don't look good. *Managing diversity just means managing well.*

Remember that diversity has many faces, literally and figuratively. As a leader in your organization, you want to harness all the talent you can find. Part of your job is to set goals. You set short-term goals and long-term goals. You also set goals on a variety of levels, perhaps in terms of productivity, efficiency, or cost effectiveness. You may set goals for your organization, your division, your department, your staff and yourself. But goal setting is

1

not all you do. In fact, as a leader, your personal effectiveness is scored on the efficiency and effectiveness of the people you manage. So it naturally follows that a big part of your job, perhaps the most important part, is "growing people."

Today's reality includes a labor force that is being transformed by women and minorities. As a leader addressing excellence in the workplace, you are obliged to manage your people so that they all perform to the best of their abilities. You need to tap the rich source of human capital within the ranks by removing barriers where they exist and by helping those who may need it to achieve their highest potential. That means you want a company or branch, or department or team, in which every person feels valued and eager to give you and the organization his or her very best. Indeed, managing your diverse work force is not just a nice thing to do—it's the smart thing to do.

Of course, there are legal reasons why you have to be fair—you can get into deep trouble if someone can prove that you are not. Remember that racism and all the other "isms" are a systematic attempt to subordinate a particular group of people, and that is illegal. Legal issues aside, however, there are a number of compelling reasons to improve your management skills in this area. The first, and perhaps most important in terms of organizational survival, is for the competitive edge.

The Competitive Edge

In its search for justice, flexibility and improved productivity, an organization restructures, reorganizes and retrenches. It defines and declares a new vision. It makes a plea for fairness, opportunity and sensitivity to each employee. Yet surprisingly, everyone carries on the way they always have: business as usual.

Today's critical economic climate (the reality of tight budgets plus an ever-increasing need to do more with less) makes it painfully clear that business as usual is an unusually bad idea. Change is essential, not only in structure, but in attitude, behavior and approach. To compete, an organization needs to be more flexible and able to respond quickly to customer demands. The power within must be tapped. Individual employees have to take initiative, assume risks and be responsible and accountable. Corporately, to succeed and to surpass the competition, you must create an environment that promotes and supports each individual. If you want effective work groups or teams, you must create your own new dynamic. A bad peace can be as difficult as war; in other words, you must manage for success.

Over and over again, research shows that the more varied the group, the better the decision-making capability and the more solid and reliable the results. And still, as managers or supervisors, or simply as people, we tend to be more comfortable with "our own." As leaders with some degree of power in the organization, we often try to find staff who appear to be most like ourselves, or reflect our mirror image. Apparently, that's human nature. According to the research, however, it is also counter-productive.

If you want a customer-oriented team, you need a team that best reflects the customer. If you want a flexible staff that can quickly adjust to changing business demands, you need a variety of ideas, attitudes and approaches. If you are looking for improved productivity and efficiency, the more varied your group, the more diverse their ideas, attitudes and approaches, and the more likely you are to achieve success. And if you want a competitive edge, you are going to have to take advantage of the diversity within your work force. In fact, if you are concerned about quality management, managing diversity is key.

Quality Management

Let's be honest. Quality management, or continuous improvement, is based on the willingness of everyone involved to make a continuous effort toward making a difference. We could call that willingness *empowerment*. Empowerment is a weighty word that has been used, abused and kicked around mercilessly for a long time now. It is also a word that, while well intentioned, has been seriously maligned and misunderstood. In fact, it might qualify for the list of "most overused words of the year." Usually, empowerment is thought of like a simple commodity that can be passed around at will; continuous improvement is the natural result. Not true!

Empowerment is not something bestowed upon people. It is not a gift given or a freedom allowed. When someone thoughtfully empowers employees to be creative, to be risk takers, to be innovative, flexible or accountable, that someone may believe they are following current management dogma and may even feel pretty good about it. But the truth is that they are not really doing any empowering at all. When managers exhort their staff to strive for continuous improvement by trying harder, those managers may think they are on the cutting edge of quality management. The truth is that they may be mandating, they may be delegating, they may be requiring, authorizing, suggesting or merely asking—but they are certainly not empowering.

Empowerment is a locus of control issue; it comes from within each individual, or it simply does not exist. A sense of empowerment stems from an internal belief that "I am of value," and that belief rests firmly on the feedback I get from my environment. That feedback at work, whether spoken, written or merely implied, is usually under the control of my manager. Whether my manager believes it or not, I listen to both the clear and the coded messages being sent.

Still, behaviors such as uniformity, predictability and

conventionalism are the norm in most organizations. There is an unspoken expectation that everyone will do their best to quietly melt into the existing group, to "fit in." However, these are the attitudes and behaviors that create significant obstacles to managing diversity and to promoting individual peak performance. If "fitting in" means I must try not to be myself, how can I possibly be my best? How can I do my best? Why would I even want to, if my manager or my organization doesn't value me for who I am? For what is unique and different in me?

To manage for quality, the barriers to superior performance, originally erected to keep some people out, must be removed for everyone. It is a slow process, but one that fits right in with your job as a leader.

Leaders understand and maximize their own performance and are instrumental in doing the same for others. They help others feel significant. They respect and value the contributions of their employees and value their diversity as well. They do not accept less than an individual is capable of achieving, and they learn how to handle sensitive issues and use feedback as a growth opportunity for employees.

Quality management demands empowering leaders who participate as catalysts, encouraging involvement, contribution, creativity and risk taking. They are able to nourish employees and teams. An empowering leader "grows" people and makes certain that each individual receives training in the skills and behaviors he or she needs in order to move forward. A leader guides, counsels and coaches; a leader shares the vision and ensures that employees have the authority, as well as the mandate and responsibility, to implement decisions.

Empowered teams share in decision making and in accepting the responsibility for their decisions. In the early stages of transition, everyone participates in offering input and the leader guides the team through the process of reaching consensus. Once a decision is made, everyone accepts responsibility for the outcome. As empowerment becomes a way of life, the leader may simply charge the team with reaching a decision. It is understood that team decisions bind all members, which is strong motivation for everyone to commit to a positive outcome. An empowered team is synergistic; energy is multiplied, and individual and group power is unleashed. Everyone shares responsibility, team pride and recognition. Quality management has made it happen.

The prevailing wisdom is that there are two key ingredients for success in today's challenging business environment:

1. Managers who are effective leaders

2. Employees who are committed, valued and empowered.

A leader influences others by creating a climate conducive to empowerment for every individual; when everyone feels included, commitment, involvement and a willingness to continuously improve are the natural consequences. Leadership, a requirement of quality management, does not imply the abdication of responsibility as many fear. It does require strength, skills and energy. It requires education, a solid sense of self, a commitment to change, an ability and a desire to share the vision and, most importantly, a truckload full of good, reliable strategies.

Without all of these good things, what you have is unhappy employees. If you have unhappy employees, you don't have productive employees. If you don't have productive employees, you have dissatisfied employees. Dissatisfied employees tend to quit, and quitting costs you big. At the very least, high employee turnover costs you time and energy and talent. At worst, it may cost you your job. So if, as a manager, you hope to decrease employee turnover, you must create a supportive environment for all.

Decreasing Employee Turnover

Not surprisingly, when organizations take the time to examine the where and the why of voluntary staff turnover, they discover that the greatest employee loss is at the lower levels where, for better or for worse, affirmative action initiatives have traditionally had their greatest numerical impact. If these organizations then look beyond that superficial numbers count and scratch a little deeper, they will find that turnover is actually greatest among the very groups they were attempting to attract. If these organizations happen to use employee exit interviews to reveal the reasons why people leave, unfortunately, they are apt to get only half the story—the report that an individual just "wasn't happy" or "found a better job." Few organizations bother to find out just what those answers really mean or what they imply. If they did, they might be very surprised indeed.

Most organizations work under the illusion that people come to work for a paycheck. Well, of course they do, but that's not the only reason people continue to work where they do. In fact, research tells us that the paycheck is one of the least important factors that keeps an employee content with the job or personally invested in it. You might be stunned to discover that lots of people stay right where they are in spite of the fact that they think they could make more money elsewhere. They stay because there is something they like about working where they do. Something about it makes them feel good.

Do you know what is most important to your employees?

A list of reasons people stay with the job they have is provided in the following questionnaire. Review the list and make some educated guesses. Number the items in the order you think is realistic, from 1 (most important) to 15 (least important). Then, use the list as an opportunity to get to know your staff a little better, to find out what drives them, what makes for a contented work environment and what keeps them happy and working where they do. Use the questionnaire to find out more about your staff. The information you get will help guide you; it may very well tell you exactly where you need to begin to focus in managing diversity. You will probably learn that while everyone is different in behavior and style, there are some basic needs and central values that are universal to all. And you need to know precisely what they are. If a day without sunshine is like a night, it's up to you to cast some light.

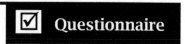

☑ Questionnaire

What Is Most Important in My Job?

The following is a list of elements most people consider when they stop to think about whether or not they are happy at work. With 1 being most important and 15 being least important, decide the order of importance to you.

_____ Convenience to where I live

_____ The pay

_____ Challenging work

_____ The company image

_____ The opportunity for personal growth

_____ The people I work with

_____ The opportunity to move up the ladder

_____ The opportunity to learn new skills

_____ The "feel" of the atmosphere

_____ The opportunity to make decisions

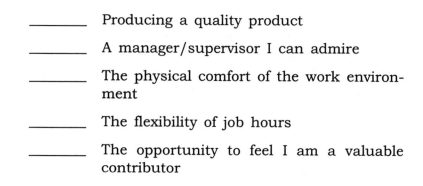

_____ Producing a quality product

_____ A manager/supervisor I can admire

_____ The physical comfort of the work environment

_____ The flexibility of job hours

_____ The opportunity to feel I am a valuable contributor

Kotter and Heskett, the dynamic investigative duo from the Harvard Business School, devote their latest best-selling textbook, *Corporate Culture and Performance*, to examining what it is that makes some corporate cultures especially successful in today's marketplace. They tell us that, to be successful, an organization must be highly responsive to:

- The shareholders

- The economic environment

- The customer

- The employees

We will assume here that you have the first three well under control, but we need to ask about the fourth: your employees. Too many organizations are simply too eager to ignore this important constituency, and as a result, things just don't work as well as they might.

If your employees are dissatisfied and apt to leave, that costs big bucks. It costs in terms of the time, energy and dollars invested in the quitter. Plus, it is expensive in terms of getting someone new. First, you have to find the someone. Then you have to train them to fill the slot, and that costs big too. Even if they come from within, they may need guidance, coaching and counseling. They may have a slow learning curve and need some time to get the hang of the job. They may also need to feel a part of the effort, and that takes time, energy and patience. Without that support, they too will become dissatisfied and leave and may even start a new trend as they close the door behind them. As a leader, you have to consider the real cost of employee turnover.

Cost Reduction

Maximum productivity, new ideas, streamlining processes and multiple skills development are all best achieved with people who are pleased to be where they are and willing to go the "extra mile." Far too many organizations donate paychecks to "on-the-job quitters," people who gave up long ago.

Organizations can no longer afford to simply "up the price" of the product they sell to make up for internal inefficiency or mediocre productivity. You can't just pass the cost of ineptitude on to the consumer and hope that nobody notices. The only way you can be competitive in today's challenging marketplace is to cut your internal costs by getting the maximum effort from everyone who collects a company check, i.e., everyone who works there. And to do that, to positively influence the behavior of the people you manage, you need to be a leader.

Leadership does not occur in isolation. Leaders have vision and are good at sharing it. They get commitment to the vision, and their management style reflects all the good things written into the vision statement. Leaders empower their people—all of their people—and encourage them to be the best they can be.

So, if you want to be a good leader rather than simply a reasonably decent bureaucratic manager, you need to develop the skills currently identified as being essential to your management tool kit. The key competencies of effective leaders are:

1. Sound judgment and good decision making

2. Vision

3. Communication skills

4. Goal setting for strategic and operational improvement

5. Change management skills

The following quick quiz will give you a bird's-eye view of how you rate. Answer the questions yes or no, and add up your scores for an indication of how you are doing in these five key competency areas. Are you following "best practices" in your management style?

 **Questionnaire**

"Best Practices" Quick Quiz

1. Decision Making

1. In the privacy of my office, I decide what the game plan is for my staff and then I make sure they all understand.
   ☐ always   ☐ usually   ☐ sometimes   ☐ never

2. I ask for information from one or two key personnel and base my decision on their input.
   ☐ always   ☐ usually   ☐ sometimes   ☐ never

3. I ask for information from my key personnel and then make my own decision based on what I think is best.
   ☐ always   ☐ usually   ☐ sometimes   ☐ never

4. My decisions are based on previous practices.
   ☐ always   ☐ usually   ☐ sometimes   ☐ never

5.   I check with my superiors before taking any new direction.

☐ always   ☐ only if I must   ☐ sometimes   ☐ never

6.   I expect that my staff will support my decisions, even if they had no input and do not agree with them.

☐ absolutely   ☐ somewhat   ☐ not really

7.   I need all the information I can get before I make up my mind.

☐ always   ☐ usually   ☐ sometimes   ☐ never

8.   I like to create a committee to gather and present all pertinent information to me before I make a decision.

☐ always   ☐ usually   ☐ sometimes   ☐ never

9.   All decisions for change require some risk or they are too safe to be useful.

☐ absolutely   ☐ somewhat   ☐ not really

10. Because I am in charge, all results rest on me. I have the right and the responsibility to do what I think is best even if my staff disagree.

☐ absolutely   ☐ somewhat   ☐ not really

2. Vision

1.   I have a picture of where the company is going and how I can help it get there.

☐ absolutely   ☐ somewhat   ☐ not really

2.   Any one of my staff could tell a stranger what my vision is.

☐ absolutely   ☐ somewhat   ☐ not really

3. Everyone on my staff understands how each person contributes to the vision.
    ☐ absolutely   ☐ somewhat   ☐ not really

4. The vision was created in consultation with my staff.
    ☐ absolutely   ☐ somewhat   ☐ not really

5. The vision incorporates the company initiatives.
    ☐ absolutely   ☐ somewhat   ☐ not really

6. I and my staff have written mission statements for short-term goals, to help us achieve the vision.
    ☐ absolutely   ☐ somewhat   ☐ not really

7. I have had consultations with my staff to help them see how their own personal vision ties into the company vision.
    ☐ absolutely   ☐ somewhat   ☐ not really

8. With my staff, I regularly review where we are on the road to our vision.
    ☐ absolutely   ☐ somewhat   ☐ not really

9. The vision is proactive, not reactive, in terms of the marketplace.
    ☐ absolutely   ☐ somewhat   ☐ not really

10. The vision includes the employees as well as a customer statement.
    ☐ absolutely   ☐ somewhat   ☐ not really

11. Our vision is posted on the wall.
    ☐ yes   ☐ no

12. We check with our customers and other departments to ensure that our vision meets their needs.
    ☐ always   ☐ usually   ☐ sometimes   ☐ never

3. Communication Skills

1. I believe that it is not my business to inquire about an employee's life outside the office.
   ☐ absolutely   ☐ somewhat   ☐ not really

2. I inform my staff of all the information they need through a flow of memos or e-mail.
   ☐ yes   ☐ no

3. I only need or want to hear about problems.
   ☐ absolutely   ☐ somewhat   ☐ not really

4. I regularly schedule one-on-one coaching meetings with all staff.
   ☐ always   ☐ usually   ☐ sometimes   ☐ never

5. I keep my personal information to myself.
   ☐ absolutely   ☐ somewhat   ☐ not really

6. I don't intend to "update" my language just to suit a few complainers.
   ☐ I do   ☐ I don't

7. Staff should solve their own conflicts.
   ☐ always   ☐ usually   ☐ sometimes   ☐ never

8. When one of my female staff seems distracted or out-of-sorts, I assume it's PMS and try to ignore it.
   ☐ always   ☐ usually   ☐ sometimes   ☐ never

9. If somebody doesn't participate the way the rest of the group does, I assume that's just "their way."
   ☐ always   ☐ usually   ☐ sometimes   ☐ never

10. I set the agenda for meetings.
    ☐ always   ☐ usually   ☐ sometimes   ☐ never

11. I like to play devil's advocate; it helps my staff develop.
    ☐ always   ☐ usually   ☐ sometimes   ☐ never

12. I never ask questions I don't know the answers to.
    ☐ I do ask   ☐ I don't ask

4. Goal Setting

1. Goals are for hockey players; we've got a job to do.
   ☐ absolutely   ☐ somewhat   ☐ not really

2. Since some groups of people are naturally limited, I set goals that I know are within easy reach.
   ☐ always   ☐ usually   ☐ sometimes   ☐ never

3. I challenge staff to come up with new methods.
   ☐ always   ☐ usually   ☐ sometimes   ☐ never

4. I don't want to hear about goals my staff think they can't achieve.
   ☐ I do ask   ☐ I don't

5. I accept the goals set for my department.
   ☐ always   ☐ usually   ☐ sometimes   ☐ never

6. I and my staff evaluate goals and reset them at regular intervals.
   ☐ always   ☐ usually   ☐ sometimes   ☐ never

7. I make sure each person's goals have developmental elements.
   ☐ always   ☐ usually   ☐ sometimes   ☐ never

8. I like my staff to decide for themselves how they will meet their goals.
   ☐ always   ☐ usually   ☐ sometimes   ☐ never

9. Our goals tie in with our vision.
    ☐ absolutely   ☐ somewhat   ☐ not really

10. If we fall short of our goals, heads will roll.
    ☐ absolutely   ☐ somewhat   ☐ not really

11. All employees have a game plan as to how they will achieve their goals.
    ☐ absolutely   ☐ somewhat   ☐ not really

12. I and my staff have had training in objective goal setting.
    ☐ absolutely   ☐ somewhat   ☐ not really

5. Change Management Skills

1. I help my employees to voice their concerns about change.
    ☐ always   ☐ usually   ☐ sometimes   ☐ never

2. I tackle issues as they arise.
    ☐ always   ☐ usually   ☐ sometimes   ☐ never

3. I encourage interim task forces or units to deal with change issues on a temporary basis.
    ☐ always   ☐ usually   ☐ sometimes   ☐ never

4. I tell my staff that mourning the past is unhealthy.
    ☐ absolutely   ☐ somewhat   ☐ not really

5. I ask for success stories at every team meeting.
    ☐ always   ☐ usually   ☐ sometimes   ☐ never

6. I do not want to hear from the skeptics or from people with weird ideas.
    ☐ I do   ☐ I don't

7. I insist that we put an end to talking about "the good ol' days."

    ☐ absolutely   ☐ somewhat   ☐ not really

8. Humor helps to deal with the stress of change.

    ☐ absolutely   ☐ somewhat   ☐ not really

9. I encourage temporary changes in the physical environment to reflect the change in structure or processes.

    ☐ absolutely   ☐ somewhat   ☐ not really

10. I have conversations with staff about what change will mean to them.

    ☐ absolutely   ☐ somewhat   ☐ not really

11. I admit to my staff that change disturbs me too.

    ☐ absolutely   ☐ somewhat   ☐ not really

12. I ask my staff for suggestions to help them manage change.

    ☐ absolutely   ☐ somewhat   ☐ not really

"Best Practices" Best Answers

1. Decision Making

1. According to research, you have only a 50% chance of arriving at the right decision on your own. Score 0 for always or usually, 2 for sometimes, 1 for never.

2. People give more to their work when they are involved in determining how the work should be done. Information should come from everyone involved. Find ways to include everyone. Score 0 for always or usually, 1 for sometimes, 2 for never.

3. Making your own decisions and ignoring input creates the potential for zero staff commitment to your decisions. Score 0 for always or usually, 2 for sometimes, 1 for never.

4. Innovation is required; value added (what your diverse group of people bring to the table) must be considered. Score 0 for always or usually, 2 for sometimes, 1 for never.

5. You need to keep your superiors informed, of course, but you should be checking with your staff who will have to move on your decision. Score 0 for always or if I must, 1 for sometimes, 2 for never.

6. Consensus decision making is always the superior route; your staff will support their own decisions. Of course, a skilled leader can influence his or her staff's decisions. Score 0 for absolutely, 1 for somewhat, 2 for not really.

7. You're wasting a lot of time; it's called paralysis by analysis. Score 0 for always or usually, 2 for sometimes, 1 for never.

8. This is a useless exercise unless the committee collects information from everybody, and unless the decision to be made is financially worth the time invested in the information gathering process. Score 0 for always or usually, 2 for sometimes, 1 for never.

9. That's generally true. Score 2 for absolutely, 1 for somewhat, 0 for not really.

10. No. Or yes if you are a one-person show. If not, you'd better educate your staff well, so they can make the decisions that will make you look good. Score 0 for absolutely, 2 for somewhat, 1 for not really.

2. Vision

1. If you don't, you're all in trouble. Score 2 for absolutely, 1 for somewhat, 0 for not really.

2. Your staff should be able to recite it by heart. Score 2 for absolutely, 1 for somewhat, 0 for not really.

3. If each person understands, they will contribute. If they do not, they are unlikely to make a significant contribution. Score 2 for absolutely, 1 for somewhat, 0 for not really.

4. Consultation is the only way to create a vision that is meaningful to all. Score 2 for absolutely, 1 for somewhat, 0 for not really.

5. It should. Score 2 for absolutely, 1 for somewhat, 0 for not really.

6. Good for you! Score 2 for absolutely, 1 for somewhat, 0 for not really.

7. It's very important to "single track" individual and corporate goals. That's what makes people feel good about going the extra mile. Score 2 for absolutely, 1 for somewhat, 0 for not really.

8. You bet! Score 2 for absolutely, 1 for somewhat, 0 for not really.

9. It is critical to be in touch with the marketplace. Score 2 for absolutely, 1 for somewhat, 0 for not really.

10. Employees count too! Score 2 for absolutely, 1 for somewhat, 0 for not really.

11. If I can't see it, it doesn't exist! Score 2 for yes, 0 for no.

12. Of course you must. Score 2 for always, 1 for usually, 0 for sometimes or never.

3. Communication Skills

1. Of course, intimate or invasive questions are always
out of bounds. But if you show no interest in your
staff's interests or life outside the office, how can
they feel valued as individuals? Just remember to
be sensitive to the fine line between good communication and prying. Be respectful. Value differences.
Score 0 for absolutely, 2 for somewhat, 0 for not
really.

2. No. Slap your hands! Get out there and talk to them.
Score 0 for yes, 2 for no.

3. What about the good stuff? What about the suc-
cesses and congratulations for the "over and above,"
the value-added opportunities you are missing. Use
the good stuff for positive feedback. Score 0 for absolutely, 1 for somewhat, 2 for not really.

4. Of course! Good for you. Score 2 for always, 1 for
usually, 0 for sometimes or never.

5. In order to trust you, they have to know you. Your
people want to know about your management style,
your personal style, your favored decision-making
process and your communication style. Score 0 for
absolutely, 1 for somewhat, 2 for not really.

6. You may have to change just to keep up. Pay attention! Complaints about outdated language (such as
calling female staff "the girls") are usually a reaction
to feeling offended or put down. Ask about the complaint. Find out what offends and why. In addition,
to manage well, your language must always be inclusive, not exclusive. Score 2 for I do, 0 for I don't.

7. That's part of your role as a counselor and coach. Win/lose situations are not healthy for staff morale. Score 0 for always or usually, 2 for sometimes, 1 for never.

8. Your bias is showing! Get more information. Find out what's going on, and respect the answers you get. Score 0 for always or usually, 0 for sometimes, 2 for never.

9. Get more information. Maybe it is a personality trait, or perhaps you are unaware of a cultural value held by an individual. Take the time to check it out. Respect the answers you get. Develop a relationship. Score 0 for always or usually, 1 for sometimes, 2 for never.

10. If the agenda is always yours, you have succeeded in building a major obstacle to running a successful meeting. What does everybody else do with the stuff they think is important? Score 0 for always, 1 for usually, 2 for sometimes, 2 for never.

11. Playing devil's advocate makes you look like the devil! If you believe there are flaws in a particular point of view, consider turning things around by asking a question such as "What might happen if this didn't work?" or "What, if anything, could go wrong if we do it that way?" Score 0 for always or usually, 2 for sometimes, 1 for never.

12. How will you learn? Score 2 for I do ask, 0 for I don't ask.

4. Goal Setting

1. No. Two-minute penalty for lunacy. Score 0 for absolutely, 1 for somewhat, 2 for not really.

2. How can your people improve if they don't stretch? Score 0 for always or usually, 1 for sometimes, 2 for never.

3. Yes. Good for you. Score 2 for always or usually, 1 for sometimes, 0 for never.

4. It's better to know the what and why so you can do some problem solving. Score 2 for I do ask, 0 for I don't.

5. Yes, within reason. But you may need to change them, adapt them or negotiate them. Score 1 for always or usually, 2 for sometimes, 0 for never.

6. Certainly. You must! Score 2 for always or usually, 1 for sometimes, 0 for never.

7. Yes. Score 2 for always or usually, 1 for sometimes, 0 for never.

8. You betcha! That's the best way to get commitment. Participative goal setting ensures both the quality and the effectiveness of results. Score 2 for always or usually, 1 for sometimes, 0 for never.

9. They'd better! Score 2 for absolutely, 1 for somewhat, 0 for not really.

10. No, no, no. Risk taking will never occur if you do that. Score 0 for absolutely, 1 for somewhat, 2 for not really.

11. Yes. And they may need your input to assist them in developing that plan. Score 2 for absolutely, 1 for somewhat, 0 for not really.

12. Yes, we have all had training in goal setting. Score 2 for absolutely, 1 for somewhat, 0 for not really.

5. Change Management Skills

1. Change is a human issue and people need to talk about it. Score 2 for always or usually, 1 for sometimes, 0 for never.

2. The tough stuff will not go away by itself, and leaving sores to fester may make things worse. Score 2 for always or usually, 1 for sometimes, 0 for never.

3. Good idea. Not only will you get good solutions, but you are "growing" your people. Besides, when you set up "temporary systems" that admit that change is a challenge, you are instantly miles ahead in managing the change itself. Score 2 for always or usually, 1 for sometimes, 0 for never.

4. Have a heart. Mourning the past is a natural, universal, human response to change. Don't wallow in the past, but put it to bed with some sort of parting ceremony or sign-off event (see Chapter 2, Creating the Motivational Climate). Score 0 for absolutely, 1 for somewhat, 2 for not really.

5. Good for you—and good for the change process. Score 2 for always or usually, 1 for sometimes, 0 for never.

6. They're out there somewhere; you might as well get them out in the open. Besides, they may actually have some good ideas. Score 2 for I do, 0 for I don't.

7. If we ignore the past, we invalidate what everyone has accomplished before now. But it can get boring, so set limits. Score 0 for absolutely, 1 for somewhat, 2 for not really.

8. You bet! Score 2 for absolutely, 1 for somewhat, 0 for not really.

9.   Temporary changes that are called "temporary" or transitional" remind people that this too shall pass. Score 2 for absolutely, 1 for somewhat, 0 for not really.

10. They need and want your support and your ear. Score 2 for absolutely, 1 for somewhat, 0 for not really.

11. Your staff needs to see that you are human too. Score 2 for absolutely, 1 for somewhat, 0 for not really.

12. Right on! Your staff may have some super ideas. Score 2 for absolutely, 1 for somewhat, 0 for not really.

Scoring

Best total possible is 116.

100–116   Superior skills. Use this book to keep building on your strengths.

80–100   Average skills. There's room for growth here. Use this book for guidance.

60–80   Your management style is out of date, out of favor or out of left field. Your ideas may be relics from the old style of "power" management which has been found to interfere with the ability to manage people—especially people who are different from you. Get some training. Read this book!

Below 60 Check your responses and sign up for any and all training you can find. Consider having long conversations with your staff about how to change your leadership style; you need to find out how your people want to be managed.

Summary

So, how sound is your judgment; how good is your ability to make decisions? Does your vision include everyone? Are your communications and goals-setting skills up to par? How well do you manage change? All of these are competencies you will need to master if you want to manage diversity, which is, after all, just good management.

If you do not have these skills, ask yourself whether the following report could have been found in your organization's newsletter?

Story

Cyclops Vision Impaired

Months of visioning, strategizing, reorganizing and right-sizing turned to calamity at the Cyclops Manufacturing Plant today, a representative of the senior management group reported to our company newsletter. "I can't understand what happened," claimed Slim Chance. "We considered it very carefully, wrote it all out, posted it on the board room wall, and communicated electronically to all the important people. Everyone should know it by heart. Apparently, they don't."

Random testing revealed that the vision was not noticed by the majority of Cyclops employees. When asked to explain it, some believed the vision statement to be an innovative eye chart. Others guessed that it was Tipper Gore's Christmas wish list. A few thought it was meant to apply to visiting dignitaries because it sure didn't speak to employees. Still others said, "Vision? I didn't see it!" Obviously, the assistance of experts is required to get the message across. But where are they? Are they you?

CREATING THE MOTIVATIONAL CLIMATE

2

Perhaps you are reading this book because it was given to you as part of your organization's commitment to building a better environment. Maybe you are reading it because you want an aid to developing yourself in a way that will increase your likelihood of being successful in a changing environment. Whatever your reason, you must first understand that people are motivated to change either because their vision of the future requires it or because compelling outside forces demand it. Change does not occur when everyone is perfectly happy with the status quo. Keeping that in mind, you must also understand climate, or culture, before you can ever hope to influence others with positive results.

In most organizations, climate, work environment or milieu are catchwords generally used interchangeably. All of these words refer to organizational *culture,* which is to say, *the way we do things around here.* Every organization has its own culture, just as every special interest group, ethnic group, family group or age group has its own culture. There are certain unwritten codes of behavior, specific silent expectations or hidden codes that set the tone and create the climate.

27

More than a decade ago, Peters and Waterman ex-
amined the corporate culture of highly successful companies in their book, *In Search of Excellence*. Peters and
Waterman evaluated the cultural elements that they believed led to the achievements of these companies and
said, essentially, that a bias for one kind of behavior over
another meant that a company was likely to be successful in a competitive arena. More recently, Kotter and
Heskett wrote *Corporate Culture and Performance*, in which
they explore the same topic with somewhat different con-
clusions. Interestingly, both of these books point out that
an organization with a strong corporate culture, demonstrating specific positive characteristics, is more likely to
be successful (no matter how you measure success) than
a company lacking these characteristics. Indeed, the organizations discussed in both of these books are typical
of organizations that are able to support diversity initiatives because of their deep cultural bias for flexibility, a
real concern for people (customers, stakeholders and employees) and a willingness to take calculated risks.

Well, you may ask, what does climate or culture have
to do with managing diversity? The answer is—just about
everything. But before you go off half-cocked about your
own organization's commitment to diversity initiatives, you
will have to explore a little more deeply. Are your leaders
just talking the talk? Or are they walking the walk? In
other words, are the powers that be simply paying lip
service to the ethics of a "new age," or are they and you
really in a position to make substantial progress towards
the changes you envision?

To get the picture, you will need a culture inventory
that measures diversity awareness and sensitivity and
answers the following questions:

- What do we look like?

- What do we want to look like?

While it is possible to mandate acceptable tolerance
levels or behaviors, to do more, and benefit on a variety

of levels by tapping a new and rich natural resource, it is imperative to know where your organization now stands and to look closely at the motivating forces behind the current culture. The hidden requirements or secret codes for inclusion and the implicit values that drive the organization must be determined. The kinds of behavior that are presently being rewarded must be discovered. You need to reveal the unwritten rules that determine who will have access to power and who will be excluded, if you are to manage your diverse work force well.

Once you have an idea of what your culture looks like, you are in a position to determine what behaviors and systems need to change.

Most organizations want to go beyond the legal basics and are philosophically dedicated to achieving the ideal, i.e., realizing a work force that, at every level, reflects the community. These same organizations are also realistically terrified when forced to confront themselves. While it is true that most of us are inherently fair and decent people, our profoundly European-based social system often blinds us to the pervasive impact of that Eurocentric point of view on our perception of others. We may be afraid to discover how biased or narrow we really are.

Discovery Through Measurement

In *The New Rational Manager,* Kepner and Tragoe write, "Everyone agrees that there is room for improvement, that the organization as we know it is not perfect. Failure of the organization to perform as a functional unit limits full realization of its potential." To promote peak performance of every involved individual, an organization must create an environment in which, without regard to race, gender, age, physical challenge or ethnicity, each and every employee has equal access to and opportunity for personal and organizational success. To ensure maximum commitment, ownership and achievement, an organization requires a climate or culture that eliminates systemic barriers (blocks within the corporate system), not only because it is the nice thing to do, but because it is the smart thing to do. When it is important to do more with less, maximizing human capital makes good business sense. Moreover, as Michael Crawford points out in his thoughtful article on race and gender in the May 1993 edition of *Canadian Business*, "The rules for workplace conduct keep being rewritten, thanks to the increasing presence of women and minorities."

By now you should be asking, "Where do I find an instrument to measure my corporate culture?" Numerous instruments are available, some are excellent and some less so. Few of them actually tackle culture from a diversity perspective, but if you search the market, you will find some that do. You would use such an instrument to measure what your organization looks like right now and compare your findings to what it would look like "ideally," or in the perfect world.

A number of instruments, such as the *Diversity Awareness Profile* by Karen Grote, are available from Pfeiffer and Company. The Grote instrument is quick and easy and certainly adequate for individual testing, but you will have to do some averaging of final test scores (which may require a loss of confidentiality) to get an idea of what your corporate culture is actually like. University Associates, Inc. publishes a useful series of annuals which may also provide instruments you can use.

Another alternative is to simply use the following questionnaire. Pass it out to your team members and ask that they complete it in five minutes. Promise them confidentiality and remind them not to sign their names. The information you receive will help you focus on specifics. Repeat the questionnaire every six to nine months to keep yourself updated.

Use the answers to the *extra question* to stimulate discussion and to problem solve.

☑ **Questionnaire**

Culture Inventory

1. Everyone around here usually gets a fair break regardless of age, appearance, ethnicity or background.

2. Everyone is offered an equal opportunity for personal growth most of the time.

3. Everyone is offered an equal opportunity for professional development most of the time.

4. Just about everyone knows that the organization will not tolerate racism, sexism or any other "ism."

5. Special celebration days or events usually consider the interests and sensitivities of all members. (For example, nobody around here would send a strip-o-gram as an office birthday surprise, or nobody would suggest we serve pork as the only entrée at the annual awards ceremony.)

6. Everyone is included in decisions that affect them if at all possible.

7. Almost everyone is comfortable about educating the rest of us about who they are and how their "difference" is important to them.

8. Everyone is comfortable pointing out any areas for improvement.

9. Just about everyone firmly believes that the organization values their individual contribution.

10. Everyone is respectful of everyone else most of the time.

11. Communication flows in many directions, so everyone usually feels included.

12. The language used around here, whether written or spoken, is always inclusive and not exclusive. (For example, "he" would not be used in a memo as the pronoun of indeterminate gender for all managers.)

Extra question: Are there incidents that stand out in your mind as exceptions to your answers?

Scoring

In a perfect world, every question should be answered yes. A perfect score is your organization's "ideal."

If your people score the organization at 8 or more, you know you are on the right track.

Between 6 and 8, you have some work to do. Examine the areas of the "no's" to give you an idea of where to begin.

A score of less than 6 indicates that you need a major shift in culture. If your organization is not on the right track, at least *you* are headed towards the light.

Interpreting Results

Questions 1 to 5 are about overt prejudice or bias. If these have been answered no, start looking for conspicuous or subtle signs of unfairness, bigotry or insensitivity that have been allowed to go unchallenged. Make immediate, clear and obvious changes.

Questions 6 to 10 are about empowerment and feeling valued as a person. If these have been answered no, your culture is probably a disempowering one, and that often results in fearful, non-risk-taking approaches to doing business. Examine your decision-making processes, your team structure and your operations processes. Start "growing" your people with coaching and counseling. Begin opening the dialogue with education. Broaden your team's skill base and their responsibility for goal achievement. Transfer power.

Questions 11 to 12 are about the power structure in your organization. If the old, hierarchical structure is alive and well where you work, information is sure to be hoarded at the top. If information is power, when information is withheld, everybody below the privileged layer is reminded of their powerlessness. Moreover, they feel that they and their efforts are undervalued, that their contributions are discounted and that they might be better off somewhere else. People who feel belittled in this way, who feel demeaned and powerless, are not about to be superior performers; they do what they must to keep their job, but they save their real energy for something else, something that nourishes them as individuals.

Even in a conventional pyramidal hierarchy, you can make a serious difference by examining how you manage your team. Look at the structure you have in place. Determine how and where you might begin to "flatten" the power structure in your department or among your immediate reports. Consider rotating leadership roles. Ask the team to create meeting agendas. Blur the lines a bit. Sharing responsibility does not mean a loss of power; it means a release of energy!

Discuss your culture inventory discoveries with your team and ask for input. Ask for suggestions. Ask for comments. Ask for reactions. Ask for help.

Now that your team has completed a culture inventory, what have you got? How can you fix it? Improve it? Give it a complete overhaul?

The culture one uncovers through a culture inventory is almost always a reflection of (or a response to) the leader at the top. At some point, in some mysterious or obvious way, the original leader set the framework within which the organization would proceed. He or she fixed the style for "the way we do things around here" as surely as cement fixes a fence post. A new leader does not, de facto, create a culture change unless that is paramount on the leader's agenda and is forcefully and noisily begun within milliseconds of the new leader taking charge. Otherwise, the culture is bound to stay very much the same as it was in the organization's infancy stage.

Decoding Your Corporate Culture

Sometimes, a corporate culture is not obvious to the people who work there every day. Even when you see the results of a culture inventory, you may not know how these results could possibly have come about, given your own commitment to change and the explicit statements of senior management. The failure to make real culture change, in spite of senior management's statements to the contrary, may simply be a case of "talking the talk" but not "walking the walk," i.e., merely paying lip service to culture change. Messages may be hidden in policies, physical layout and behaviors. These messages need to be decoded in order to discover the true nature of your culture.

In the following **translation table,** a list of attributes is given on the left. On the right is an interpretation of these attributes. You or your group may disagree with these interpretations, but what is important is how the messages are perceived by your workers. Use the table to open the discussion.

What we do	*What it says about us*
Support staff work in cubicles	Privacy is not important for support staff. Support staff are cogs in a wheel. Support staff are ex-

What we do	*What it says about us*
	pected to respond to anyone who wanders past. Support staff don't need sunlight; they are mushrooms!
Nothing personal is permitted on desks.	Our people are not individuals. There is no life outside of work worth thinking about on the job. We must all be as similar as we can be.
"Calendar girls/boys" are posted on the wall.	A sexual element is permitted in the workplace. Women or men may be demeaned. Looks are important.
The office is on the 65th floor.	We are powerful; it is important that people see us as being powerful.
There is an escort to the parking lot.	We care about our people's safety.
We have reserved parking spaces/dining rooms/window offices for our senior staff.	All animals are equal, but some are more equal than others.
Our elevator buttons are low.	Wheelchair access is important to us. It is important that everyone be able to use the office equally.
We served pork at the Christmas party.	We don't care about your religious dietary restrictions. Christmas is the only holiday worth celebrating.
We offered a choice of entrées at our holiday celebration.	We respect differences. We chose a convenient date for all of us to celebrate the various holidays at the end of the calendar year.

What we do	*What it says about us*
We call the women at the front desk "the girls."	By using words that describe children, we keep women in their place!
Only women get leave after the birth of a child.	It's a woman's job to raise the kids.
Our work force reflects the demographics of our community.	Our company is part of the community. We need to be representative in order to better relate to our clients and to make our employees feel at home.
Everyone gets a regular update of our company's progress.	Everyone is on the team; everyone should participate in our wins and losses.
We will pay for our employees to upgrade their skills.	Just as the company is expected to grow and prosper, employees are entitled to make the most of their lives and potentials.
Our company provides same-sex spousal benefits.	We recognize that families come in different forms. We respect relationships of commitment. We could lose out on hiring a lot of good people if we ignore their needs.
We have a daycare program.	In most cases, both parents work. We know that to get the best people performing the best work, we must ensure that their children are taken care of.
Our chairs come in a variety of widths.	Some people are larger than others.

Scan your workplace for other "silent" messages. What about dress codes? Work hours? Washroom facilities? What does it all mean? Ask your team to decode the messages. Agree to begin making change.

If the change you envision is to be successful, if you are banking on valuing diversity for moral and human reward, you need to be a manager who will help build a culture in which every individual assumes personal responsibility for goal achievement; every person every day must feel accountable for shooting at the same target. Focus must be on equitable outcomes; results must be built into the plan.

Perhaps that is exactly what you intend, but in goal setting, evaluating, and counseling and coaching, you need to have some good ideas and some reliable tools to help you create the empowered and happy work force you want. If you do not, you are more likely to succeed in cultivating a solid group of superior followers who will work like crazy to "fit in" and maintain the status quo.

Until now, organizations may have been successful by having everyone fall in line. Followers, however, do not initiate change, nor do they champion innovation or accountability. Whether they be service providers or the internal keepers of the flame, followers simply do what is expected. They succeed in doing things the way they have always done them; they perform adequately within the same parameters and paradigms set by the early founders. And that attitude and those behaviors will not create the momentum for the depth of culture change a serious diversity initiative requires.

As stated by Robert Hughes (*Time Magazine*, February 1993), our future "in a globalized economy without a cold war, will rest with people who can think and act with informed grace across ethnic, cultural, and linguistic lines....In the world that is coming, if you can't manage differences, you've had it."

It would seem that training for "informed grace" is the solution of choice. But if training were all that was necessary for culture change, simple, straightforward train-ing would work. Clearly, today's training mania is costing big bucks, yet intensive follow-up studies routinely indi-cate trouble. Traditional training events seldom do more than entertain or provide an interesting "training event." There is little demonstrable relationship between training investment and real life pay-off—unless you do it right, as an integral element of a carefully linked series of results-driven steps.

The Four-Step Solution

- Step 1 is key. Measure the current culture and identify the gap between the present culture and the ideal state. (You've already done that.)

- Step 2 is motivating for awareness, sensitivity and behavior change, linking department or organiza-tional goals with individual change management strategies and personal development.

- Step 3 is implementation of ongoing support and nourishment mechanisms encompassing focus groups, ritualizing losses, offering celebration op-portunities and rethinking your reward system to include credit for demonstrated behavior change.

- Step 4 is follow-up. Keep up all the good stuff and keep going.

All four steps are necessary components for success-ful change. It is simply not good enough to send everyone off to a classroom and hope for the best. Of course train-ing is a piece, but only a small piece of what culture change is all about.

To effect real change and to strategically move every-one towards that carefully considered organizational vision, several key pieces must be in place and meticulously aligned. Once the goals are set, the "ideal" behaviors (as outlined in the organizational culture inventory you completed) necessary for the achievement of those goals must be identified. These ideal behaviors are then compared with the behaviors presently forming the organizational culture. This identifies the gap that marks your starting point, the yawning chasm you must successfully cross. It is the discrepancy between where you are and where you need to go, to achieve the defined and desired results.

Now begins the real work of seriously supporting the change initiative. At this point, the task is to link the department or organizational goals and the ideal individual behaviors necessary to achieving those goals. You may want to use a detailed individual assessment instrument to have your team members assess their on-the-job behaviors and to discover what attitudinal and behavioral modifications are necessary for goal achievement. On the other hand, you may choose to do this informally through discussion groups, committees or just by using the team-building exercises in Chapter 7.

After you have gathered your information, develop a set of specific action steps which focus on desired results. The result is that everyone is working towards moving themselves forward in pursuit of a shared vision.

Next, investigate your support mechanisms. What are you doing to ensure that the change initiative takes root? The best place to look first is the current internal reward system; it is the most obvious and solid evidence of reward and punishment—the performance evaluation system. Examine it carefully and ask yourself the following questions:

- Does it reward for challenging the system when an injustice is observed?

- How does it involve the employee?

- Does it "punish" an employee who takes personal time for a religious holiday you've never heard of?

- Does it require him or her to take personal responsibility for setting performance and behavior goals and for deciding what measurements will be accepted as valid?

- Does it value individual differences?

- Exactly what does it reward?

- What can be done to improve it?

The Pay-Off

In recognizing the need for culture change, it is understood that legislation, mandates, dictums and even ideals are likely to change little but the numbers. To achieve culture change, nothing superficial will suffice. Indeed, the culture must be redesigned (i.e., the way things are done around here must change), and in so doing, it is essential to redefine expectations and requirements.

The process of linking or single-tracking personal behavior change and department goals creates a results-driven change management system that is effective in designing and defining the desired new culture. It maximizes the effectiveness of each employee and profits both the employee and the organization. The happy consequence is that individual and organizational strategies are consolidated and activated for success. While each employee develops a personal blueprint for targeting goals, the behavior styles required for success within the new culture are neatly built into the plan.

Without these steps, unfortunately, it's business as usual.

Summary

The human element is key to achieving organizational goals because a contented work force contributes to bottom-line results. A serious effort toward culture change requires an understanding of what behaviors are currently expected and which of those behaviors interfere with an egalitarian workplace. Tie these behavioral expectations to your department goals with a four-step process, and watch your culture change.

You can use the following questionnaire to help gather information. Use it in any number of ways. Copy the page, pass it around and collect the results. Use the questions to open a team meeting, as a kick-off to announce your seriousness in changing the current culture. Or use it in some ingenious way only you can think of.

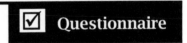
☑ Questionnaire

I Love It Here But...

1. I fit in around here because in the following way I am like everyone else. _____

   _____

2. I don't fit in around here because in the following way I am different from everyone else._____

   _____

3. When it comes to having different needs, all I ever get is _____

   _____

4. If the company cared more about people like me they would _____

    _____

5. Things would be perfect around here if only_____

    _____

6. I've heard we're trying to make things better for everyone around here. And things would be better if only _____

    _____

7. I'm so uncomfortable when _____

    _____

8. I'm sick and tired of_____

    _____

9. I could do my job better if only _____

    _____

10. I wish _____

    _____

THE LONELY SOUL

3

Believe it or not, some lucky folks have never felt what it is like to be an outsider. Some of these fortunate people just haven't got a clue. They don't understand that when a community newsletter asks for feedback on the current needs of "businessmen," there may be some successful businesswomen who are offended because they have been left out. They can't see that a newspaper report stating that "400 men in blue were sent in to quell the riot, 100 of whom were women" is not really a side-splitting typographical error. They are flabbergasted when someone objects to exchanging Christmas presents at the office (doesn't everyone celebrate Christmas?). They are apt to confide, in a rather superior or imperious tone, that they are weary of hearing the complaints of a few misguided malcontents. It's likely they really wish that those of us who insist on griping would either develop a thicker skin (and quickly), see a therapist (the sooner the better) or simply go away (quietly).

Inclusion vs. Exclusion

Most people are perfectly happy being *different* as long as they know that their difference is not perceived as a deficiency. Remember the kid with the terrific voice in your high school choir? She didn't mind being different.

She landed the coveted solo performance and the audience applauded her unique talent. Remember the boy who was the best artist in the class? He was thrilled to be different. When he drew a terrific caricature of the principal, everyone laughed uproariously and told him how clever he was. Remember the prom queen? She was ecstatic to be considered different enough to be crowned as the best. Remember the fat kid who sat sullenly at the back of the room? Now that's a different story.

What can we do with the favored individuals—the ones who just don't get it because they never had to or who, perhaps inadvertently, have contributed to a culture where being different is perceived as being deficient? Whether they intend it to or not, their confident demeanor, plus their inability to understand the very real discomfort of exclusion, makes it difficult for others to speak up or even to be themselves. (If you have to pretend to be someone else, how can you possibly do your best?) Are these "preferred" people merely dumb or has their own good fortune made them insensitive? How can we educate them, really touch them at their deepest core, so they can carry the torch instead of blowing it out?

Educate, sensitize, involve, inform—All are good ideas and all are valid. But to begin to do all of these things, start with experience.

The following is an experiential activity that offers several benefits. It will:

- Open the door to conversation

- Create an "outsider" feeling for some who have never experienced that feeling before

- Create an "insider" feeling for some who have never experienced that feeling before

- Educate and sensitize

Use the following cross-cultural experience as a workshop or experiential game. The event can take just an hour, or you can extend the training and development to a full day by choosing additional exercises from Chapter 7.

Invitation to a Cosmos Adventure

> Please join me and your fellow star travelers at an Inter-Planetary meeting to be held:
>
> Date _____
>
> Time _____
>
> Location _____
>
> We expect to enjoy an exciting and informative experience and are counting on you to attend.
>
> Captain of the Cosmos Vessel "Venture"

Objectives

To educate, sensitize, involve and inform

To open the conversation

To provide an opportunity for inclusion and exclusion

To set new behavioral goals

To have fun

Process

You are the leader, the Celebrated Captain of the Cosmos Vessel "Venture," so remember to send the invitation to all team members in advance of the big event.

Instructions

1. Divide your team into two groups. One group is from the affluent planet Goldmine. The other is from the poor but proud planet Rubble.

2. Copy and send out the invitation.

3. Dress up for the event. Choose something that indicates you are the Celebrated Captain of the Cosmos Vessel "Venture."

4. Provide colored paper or decorative items, such as ribbons, stars and crepe paper, that the two groups can use to identify themselves. If your budget allows, provide each team with identifying tee shirts or hats. The more this feels like play, the more open and involved people will become.

5. If time and money allow, run this session away from the workplace. The brighter and more welcoming the environment, the better. You will want a large, friendly room with a place for yourself at the front and two round tables for your two planetary groups to work at. You will also need three flip charts (one at the front and one for each group). Don't forget markers or pens.

6. Provide some sort of food. Breakfast or lunch is ideal. Failing that, how about some simple refreshments like coffee, tea and doughnuts?

7. Welcome everyone as they arrive at the door. Introduce yourself as the Celebrated Captain of the Cosmos Vessel "Venture."

8. If you have a preference for how the group splits up, hand out the appropriate instruction sheets as people arrive. If you prefer that the groups self-select, have the instructions waiting at the tables.

9. When everyone is seated, announce the day with something like the following:

Welcoming Address

Welcome all inter-planetary visitors. I know that you have come from far and wide to enjoy this day with new and interesting life forms, and I am most pleased that we can gather together in this way. All of us are here to help each other and to learn from each other. The future of our great and enduring cosmos is in your hands, and I wish you well with your task.

This will be a cross-cultural experience. Some of you are from the planet Goldmine and others are from Rubble. Each of you can learn valuable lessons from the other, so all that I ask is that you remember to be considerate of the strangers in your midst.

The workshop is in two parts. In Part I, you will set a strategy for your planet group. In Part II, you will interact with the other planet group.

10. At this point, it's a good idea to try to enlist your audience to spell out some goals for the session. An original way to handle that is to turn to your flip chart and ask your audience for input. Say something like, "Imagine that this session has come to a close. It's all over. When you received the invitation to this event, you never expected the day to be as incredibly super as it turned out. The workshop was unbelievably sensational. Fantastic in fact. Tell me why it was so terrific? What happened?"

    It might be helpful to tell them you are going to start them off. Write on the top of the flip chart "I liked today because." Then add something like "everyone was so open." Other good points would be things like "we all had fun" or even "it was great to get away from work and relate on a different basis." Get the group to join in.

11. When you have a half dozen or so good points on the chart, move on.

Welcoming Address Continued

Please read your instruction sheets. Spend 30 minutes deciding on your strategy. I will let you know when time is up. You will then meet with the other group to exchange ideas. Have fun!

12. Allow the group at least 30 minutes to interact in Part II. If you have more time, spend it on the debrief.

Cosmos Adventure: A Cross-Cultural Experience

The Planet Goldmine

You are from the affluent planet Goldmine. On your planet, you have everything you need to live a rich and rewarding life. You want for nothing. Still, yours is a charitable and generous society.

1. With your compatriots, decide on twelve things that make your life on Goldmine ideal and list them below.

   1. _____

   2. _____

   3. _____

   4. _____

   5. _____

   6. _____

7. _____

8. _____

9. _____

10. _____

11. _____

12. _____

2. You are about to meet with members of the poor but proud planet Rubble. With your compatriots, plan on four things you would like to teach them to improve their lives.

3. Decide how you will teach the people of Rubble without offending their pride.

4. Keeping in mind that the people of Rubble are poor but proud, carefully decide on a gift you will give them. Draw the gift on the flip chart or create it with the supplies at hand and present it to the people of Rubble when you meet.

Cosmos Adventure: A Cross Cultural-Experience

The Planet Rubble

You are from the poor but proud planet Rubble. On your planet, life is hard. You have few of the concrete things some might consider necessary to live a rich and rewarding life, but you have each other and you have your pride.

1. With your compatriots, decide on twelve things that make your life on Rubble so difficult and list them below.

1. _____

2. _____

3. _____

4. _____

5. _____

6. _____

7. _____

8. _____

9. _____

10. _____

11. _____

12. _____

2. You are about to meet with members of the affluent planet Goldmine. With your compatriots, plan on four things you would like to know that would help you to improve your lives.

3. Decide how you will ask the people of Goldmine for help without demeaning yourselves.

4. Keeping in mind that the people of Goldmine are affluent and have just about everything anyone could possibly want, carefully decide on a gift you will give them. Draw the gift on the flip chart or create it with the supplies at hand and present it to the people of Goldmine.

Instructions Continued

13. After 30 minutes, call the groups to order and tell them that the time has come to meet the other planetary group. Remind them they have 30 minutes for the activity, and suggest again that they have fun.

14. When the next 30 minutes is over, ask everyone to pull their seats into a semi-circle at the front and discuss the following questions. (If you wish, you may take notes on the flip chart or ask for a volunteer to take notes.)

Cosmos Adventure Debrief

1. What did you learn from this experience?

2. Tell me what it felt like to be an outsider?

3. What did it feel like to be an insider?

4. What did you learn about values?

5. What did you learn about sensitivity?

6. What did you learn that was uplifting?

7. What did you learn that was upsetting?

8. How can you use what you learned back on the job?

9. What was a central lesson of this experience for you?

10. What would you like to do next to help our culture change?

The Cosmos Adventure is a great idea. It's fun, it's a terrific team builder and it helps to get everyone talking the same language. Plus, it helps to focus and define the new direction. But there's more.

While some people feel included everywhere, some do not. And exclusion is an awfully lonely island. One good place to begin ensuring that everyone feels included is by using inclusive language. It is not good enough to be politically correct yourself and permit others over whom you have some influence to be thoughtless, insensitive or downright insulting in their language and humor. You must set the clear expectation that everyone, from now on, think about the implications of the language they use. After all, words are the clearest method we have of sending messages. We use words to communicate not just what we think, but also to convey how we think.

You have decided that culture change is important. You want everyone to understand that equity in the work-place is an important value. It is what makes everyone feel a part of the team. Insolence, insensitivity and exclusion will not be tolerated. How do you remind everyone of the new state of affairs?

You could start by sending around the following page as an information memo, detailing instructions for all future writing tasks.

 Memo

Avoid Sexist Writing

Good business writing requires both clarity of thought and attention to detail. Today, more than ever, people may be offended by sexist words and images.

The following are examples of ways you can eliminate sexual stereotyping:

- If you do not know the sex of the addressee, begin your letter with "Dear" followed by the initials and surname.

- When the names of a woman and man are mentioned together, use parallel language so that women are portrayed as equals:

  John Brown and Maria Perini

  J. Brown and M. Perini

- Ensure parallel treatment of couples:

  Carlos and Oosha Sanchez

  Mr. and Mrs. Carlos and Oosha Sanchez

  Mr. and Mrs. Sanchez

- Ensure parallel treatment of work associates:

  Maureen Gold and her assistant Gerry Green

  Ms. Gold and her assistant Mr. Green

- Alternate reference so that women are not always given second place. Good writers look for ways to avoid using "he" as the pronoun of indeterminate gender.

  ✓ Eliminate the pronoun

  ✓ Pluralize the pronoun

  ✓ Repeat the noun

Let's take the gender issue one step further. If you want to get some real insights into gender differences and open up a lively conversation, pass around the next little eye-opener. Give Part A to the men only and Part B to the women only. Then, in a combined group session, ask them to trade papers. Then start talking.

A. For Men Only

1. If a stranger called me "dear," I would feel _____

    _____

    _____

2. "Lady" is a word I would use to describe _____

    _____

    _____

3. When I use the word "girl" I am referring to_____

    _____

    _____

4. When I say "boy" I mean _____

    _____

    _____

5. "Women" is a word I ☐ am comfortable/☐ am not comfortable using in everyday conversation. It implies

    _____

    _____

6. I call a man "sir" when_____

    _____

    _____

7. I call a woman "ma'am" when _____

    _____

    _____

B. For Women Only

1. If a stranger called me "dear," I would feel _____

    _____

    _____

2. "Lady" is a word I would use to describe _____

    _____

    _____

3. When I use the word "girl" I am referring to_____

    _____

    _____

4. When I say "boy" I mean _____

    _____

    _____

5. "Women" is a word I ☐ am comfortable/☐ am not comfortable using in everyday conversation. It implies

    _____

    _____

6. I call a man "sir" when _____

    _____

    _____

7. I call a woman "ma'am" when _____

    _____

    _____

Clearly, what you say and what you write are not all there is to creating a culture in which everyone feels included. Some additional suggestions for including everyone and creating a culture of open and easy interaction are provided next. Not all of them will be right for you or your organization, but the list will get you started thinking. Ask your team for other ideas.

Bright Idea

Ideas for Creating Pockets of Sanity

1. Hang up a calendar and write in **every holiday** celebrated by **every person** on your team.

2. Have a "pot luck" breakfast/lunch/dinner/party and ask everyone to bring one dish that best represents their ethnic or historical background.

3. Get some educational videos from your human resources department and show them to your group at lunch time.

4. Tell your team the story of how your family came to this country. Set aside five minutes in meetings or a weekly "coffee break" session for each member of your team to tell the story of their family's or their own arrival in this country.

5. Ask each member of your team to bring in a brochure or newsletter from a service organization or religious institution to which they belong.

6. Spend some time discussing the meaning and implications of the word "handicapped."

7. Ask your team for specific ideas that would make your building/department more accessible. Attempt to implement the ideas.

8. Start a series of "celebrations" to honor specific events in the lives of your team members. Ask them to collect a possible list.

9. Get a picture of the demographics of your community. Find out more about the groups that are under-represented in your work force.

10. Once a month, once a quarter or once a year, eat at an ethnic restaurant with your team. Use the opportunity to learn more about a particular culture or just for team building.

Creating Trust

As hard as you may try, simply demanding a culture change will not make it happen. Affirmative action initiatives have managed to drive some changes through, but not always smoothly. Affirmative action sets rules and standards we must follow whether or not we favor them. Indeed, whatever personal view one may hold, in a business environment, opposing views must be suspended to get on with the business of doing business; a person must be able to handle his or her job irrespective of which side of the line he or she falls on.

We know that any change creates discomfort. Some people will be angry; they were perfectly happy the way things were. Others will be disbelieving; they've heard the same song and dance from other drum beaters before you about all the benefits that will ensue, and nothing ever really changed. Still others will feel threatened, worried that their privacy will be invaded or their "difference" come back to haunt them when the dust finally settles. *The change you envision can and will only occur when there is trust.*

The first, most basic rule about trust is that openness is a requirement. It is a universal reality that humans like and trust best people they know best; humans distrust strangers (so do dogs for that matter.) Since you, as the leader, are modeling the behaviors and attitudes you want your team to emulate, openness begins with you.

·Secrecy engenders more than distrust. Just as the universe abhors a vacuum, an absence of information sucks up fear and disinformation. It can create a whirling eddy of general discomfort. Your team wants to know who you are, not just at work, but in real life, as a person. You don't have to tell anyone your secrets. No one really needs to know about your marital problems or your no-good, pain-in-the-neck brother-in-law. It is not necessary to submit your bio to the group (although that's not a bad idea), but in some small way, every day, allow your crew some insight into you as a person—the real you, warts and all.

Enigmatically, trust is the intangible "thing" that is actually the first solid building block for an equitable and supportive culture. Trust grows from the following management competencies.

Good Communication

For communication to be good, it is simply not good enough to be articulate. Even if you write the most brilliant memos on the face of the planet, if you fail to listen, you are a good writer and a poor communicator. Conversely, you may be a less than adequate writer or speaker and still be a great communicator. Communication is a two-way street: from you and to you. Good communication in a group setting requires a flow of information in a multitude of directions, to and from everyone included in that group.

There is more to communication than just an exchange of information. Communication requires the cognitive process of digesting the information received and using that information in some way. Asking for feedback and then ignoring what you have heard is hearing, not listening. Listening requires that you hear, show that you hear (using all those good body language messages you learned in Interpersonal Skills 101) and, in some way, integrating the information you have heard into what you think, do or say next.

Without good communication, trust withers and dies on the vine.

Shared Information

When you learn something important, positive or negative, it is incumbent upon you to share the information. In every organization, the grapevine is thick and thriving. If you have heard something, someone else has probably heard it too. Or misheard it. Preempt gossip, sagging morale or ill-placed excitement with accurate information. Sharing information builds trust.

Shared Decision Making

This is the part that really puts a scare into the old-style manager. For some reason, there is a fear that if you share decision making, you won't be needed. Perhaps the decisions your people make will be inferior to the ones you would have made, or you will look weak. That's nonsense.

Research consistently demonstrates that group decisions are invariably superior to decisions made by an individual. They are better in terms of the quality of the decision and the support the decision receives from the people who must implement it. Unless time is of the essence, you are always better off sharing the decision-making process.

Of course, there are levels of sharing the decision making. The higher the level, the better the decision will be. Depending on your own comfort and the skill of your people, you may want to start at the bottom step and move up the ladder slowly, or begin at the top where the best decisions are made.

Decision-Making Levels

Level 1:   You make all the decisions yourself, based on the information you have, your organization's conventional practices and what you think best. You ask for commitment to your decision.

Level 2:   You provide information and ask for feedback from your team. You thank everyone for their feedback and make the decision yourself. You ask for commitment to your decision.

Level 3:   You provide information and ask for feedback from your team. You consider the feedback, integrate it into your thought processes, and make the decision yourself. You ask for commitment to your decision.

Level 4:   You provide all salient information and ask for feedback from your team. You and your team make the decision together, with you strongly influencing the outcome. You ask for commitment to the decision. (You may be, at this level, coaching for independent decision making.)

Level 5:   You provide all salient information and ask your team to make the decision. You agree to abide by the decision and support it, plus, you ask for commitment to the decision. And you get it!

Keeping Commitments

Your elders taught you the importance of this many years ago. There is nothing further to add to their words of wisdom.

Holding People Accountable

This means what it says. As a supervisor or manager, it is your job to help people set goals, provide coaching where it is needed and then hold people accountable for keeping their commitments. You have to be willing to bench a player who is batting zero.

Healing Souls

To heal a lost soul usually requires mentoring or counseling (detailed in Chapter 4). It always requires your sensitivity to the situation, the culture, the person and the emotions engendered by isolation. While idle chatter has it that the workplace is no place for emotions, the truth is that when you are working with people, emotions are impossible to avoid. In fact, don't even try. Instead, either on a one-to-one basis or in a safe and trusting environment, attempt to get the feelings out so that you can deal with them, move forward, set feelings aside and then go on to tackle the facts of the situation.

Improving communication, transferring responsibility, empowering and sharing decision making are all reliable routes to shepherding everyone into the same corral. It may also be a kindness to "piggy-back" a lost soul with someone you can trust to gently guide them into the group. Create a trusting culture in which lost souls are a thing of the past.

Since trust is an essential element of teamwork and productivity, it may be a good idea to show everyone on your team how important trust is in the workplace. The following is a great exercise to use in any way you wish.

Simulation

Diamonds in the Rough

Objectives

To educate, sensitize, involve and inform

To open the conversation

To set new behavioral goals

To build the team

To have fun

Process

This game works best with groups of at least five to six participants each.

1. Divide your players into groups and provide flip charts, paper and pens.

2. Tell everyone that there may be a saboteur in their group and that person will be notified of their role privately.

3. Tell everyone that the saboteur will attempt to be very cunning and will try to ruin their plans in some subtle way. Tell the group that if they identify the saboteur, the group may ask that person to leave and the person must go if asked to do so.

4. Take every player aside individually and give each a folded piece of paper that says: You are not the saboteur.

5. Tell everyone that they have 30 minutes to come up with a plan.

6. At the end of the 30 minutes, debrief the game.

7. Give the following instructions.

Instructions

For months, you have been traveling the foothills of the Cascade Mountains on burros, probing for treasure. After exhausting and fruitless exploration, you have finally uncovered the cache for which you were searching: Diamonds in the Rough.

These precious stones were hidden in 1810 by Sidewinder Sam, whose distant descendants are now secretly offering a reward of 10 million dollars to the individual who brings them back to the family.

The diamonds were buried in an old but sturdy steamer trunk, deep in the treacherous hills. They are worth at least 20 million dollars on the open market, and there is no proof that they belong to any of Sidewinder Sam's rich relatives.

If you succeed in getting the diamonds back to the office, you will share equally in the profits and be honored by our CEO at a special gala dinner.

Using the map provided, you must figure out a way to get the trunk out of the hills and back to the office without attracting attention. You know that there are bound to be robbers on the way, and since you are traveling on burros, hiding the trunk will not be easy. What's worse, you believe there may be a scoundrel in your midst who has made nefarious plans to have the diamonds hijacked en route so that the rogue can claim the 10 million dollar reward alone.

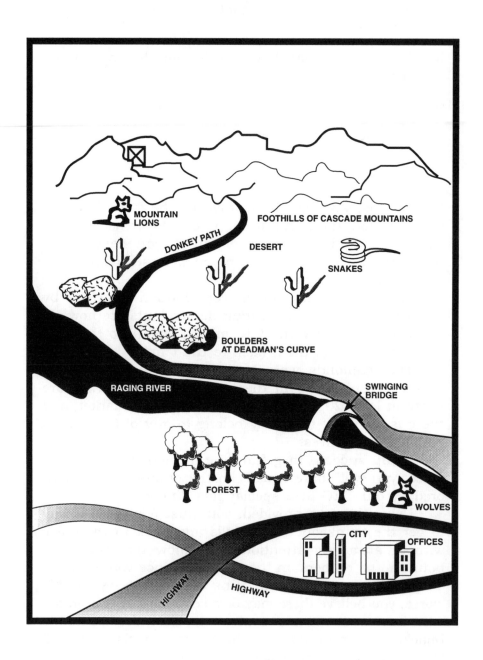

Decide how you will get the trunk back to the office. If, while you are making your plans, you discover the saboteur among you, you may vote about what to do with the rascal.

Fresh water is plentiful and you have brought along sufficient freeze-dried food for a month, so you need not worry about nourishment. In addition to your burros and trekking equipment, you also have with you:

- A bedroll for each team member

- A tent for the team

- One pot, two frying pans, a coffee maker, enough cups for each member and a knife-fork-spoon combination for each member

- One carving and gutting knife

- Two fishing rods

- Enough matches to start as many fires as you need

- One canteen per person

- One handgun for the safety of the group

- The clothes you are wearing (including a hat) plus one windbreaker per person

Debrief

1. What did you learn from this experience?

2. Did you find your saboteur?

3. What made you think that person was the saboteur?

4. What did you learn about trust?

5. What did you learn about distrust?

6. What do you think increases feelings of trust?

7. What do you think decreases feelings of trust?

8. How does distrust manifest itself around here?

9. How can you use what you learned back on the job?

10. What was a central lesson of this experience for you?

11. What does distrust do to our ability to get results?

12. If you identified the wrong saboteur, how do you feel about it?

13. How does the wrongly accused person feel?

14. If you identified no one as the saboteur, but managed to work around your suspicions, how did that affect your ability to relate to each other?

15. What would you like to do next to help our culture change?

DEVELOPING PEOPLE

4

Developing people requires solid leadership competencies because in people, as in plants, you reap what you sow (except for the odd weed that stubbornly pops up uninvited—in the garden and in the workplace). As a supervisor or manager, your behaviors and your abilities have a major influence on the immediate environment of the people who report to you.

To review then, the key competencies of effective leaders are:

1. Sound judgment and good decision making

2. Vision

3. Communication skills

4. Goal setting for strategic and operational improvement

5. Change management skills

Decision Making

For superior decision-making capabilities, both you and your staff should have training in decision-making skills. As leader, you must encourage a variety of creative decision-making approaches and respect the opinions of others, even if they differ from your own. Remember, the best decisions are made by a number of people (the more diverse, the better). Good decisions are based on a body of salient information, and you, as leader, must support the decisions of your people.

Vision

A leader with vision has a picture of where the company is going and an understanding of how to help the organization get there. Everyone on your staff should be conversant enough with your organizational vision that they could tell a stranger what it is. Moreover, everyone needs to understand how each person contributes to the vision. To stimulate everyone to participate actively in achieving the organizational vision, it is wise to create a vision for your team. To do so puts your team's role in proper perspective and creates a blueprint for successful achievement.

A strong vision is created in consultation with your staff and incorporates the company initiatives. The vision is proactive, not reactive to the marketplace, and it includes the employees as well as a customer statement.

As leader, you will regularly review where you are on the road to achieving the vision. Clarity of the vision improves when it is posted on the wall and when there are written mission statements for short-term goals to help everyone achieve the vision. Consultations with your staff also help them see how their own personal vision ties into the company vision.

Note: People may produce adequate work because they are forced to do so. People produce superior work because they **want** to do so. A job is only a job, unless the team member sees himself or herself as an essential player in the big game.

Communication Skills

Superior communication requires an information flow in as many directions as there are people. But that's not all.

An outstanding leader communicates on many levels, which is why the highly effective style of *walk-around management* is such a hot topic at senior management conferences. It takes some friendly chit-chat to really establish rapport, even at work. Relationships are key; affiliation is paramount. How else can you inquire about an employee's life outside the office, find out what new rumor is taking seed as it drops from the grapevine, or learn what's getting in the way of your group's ultimate success? How can you let your people get to know the real you except through honest, human conversation?

Superior communication also requires regularly scheduled one-on-one coaching meetings with all staff. It takes a sensitivity to people and to language to ensure that communication is inclusive; it requires a willingness to be a mediator when conflicts arise.

Your staff will be happier if:

- They know what you think

- They understand the goals

- They believe they are valued

- They are challenged to be their best

- They are given **constructive feedback** on progress.

Superior communication demands conversation, not speeches. Be open to new ideas and "different" ways of getting things done. Let others set the agenda. Ask questions to provoke discussion. Admit it when you do not have the answers; ask for help. Be a leader, not a commander.

Goal Setting

Good goal setting requires that you involve your staff in setting stretch goals. Ask them individually and as a group to decide for themselves how they will meet their goals. Make sure each person's goals have developmental elements. Listen to your staff; hear where people are confident and where they are insecure so you can respond appropriately. Challenge everyone to come up with new methods; evaluate goals and reset them at regular intervals.

Worthwhile goals tie in with your vision. Be sure that all employees have a game plan as to how they will achieve their goals (use the Action Plan in Chapter 9). If appropriate, provide training in objective goal setting.

Change Management Skills

The ability to manage change requires, first, that you acknowledge change is occurring; second, that you acknowledge the very real stress and anxiety that change usually creates; and third, that you take visible steps to allow your people to grieve for the past, ventilate fears about the present and plan for the future.

Helping employees to voice their concerns about change is important. It is also important, within reason, to tackle issues as they arise instead of allowing them to fester. Don't be afraid to have conversations with staff about what change will mean to them. Be honest enough to admit that change disturbs you too.

While all of this is going on, take the proverbial bull by the horns and make some changes of your own, changes to indicate that you too take this change thing seriously. Perhaps you will want to set up interim task forces or units to deal with change issues on a temporary basis. You might encourage temporary changes in the physical environment to reflect the change in structure or processes. Until the new structure or process is carved in granite, you may want to ask the team how they would like to handle the situation temporarily.

Change the usual meeting agenda to reflect that even in the hurricane of change swirling around you, you are making progress; ask for success stories at every team meeting. Use humor to help deal with the stress of change; circulate your own quick comics, or ask for contributions to your new "no-newsletter." Ask your staff for suggestions to help them manage change. And listen, even to the skeptics and people with weird ideas. Equally important, polish your coaching skills.

Coaching

Good management requires the ability to influence. Managers often influence through coaching, which is a **two-way conversation** that focuses on **the process for improving performance**.

Industrial psychologists are in agreement: employee commitment is essential to securing sustained superior performance. Managers are responsible for producing superior performance **through the efforts of others**. You must understand that good coaching is not demonstrating and it is not telling, nor is it delegating, ordering or sending someone off to watch somebody else. Coaching is a conversation with specific steps designed to help the learner teach himself or herself.

Dennis Kinlaw, author of *Coaching for Commitment*, stresses that there is "a major shift in management philosophy from managing by control toward managing by commitment. All the major strategies that have improved performance in this country over the past 10 years have this in common: they all have increased employee commitment to quality and productivity."

Coaching is successful if it:

- Impacts accomplishment
- Is goal-oriented
- Communicates respect
- Creates a positive working relationship
- Follows a specific series of steps

Although there are no guaranteed ways to change another's behavior, it is possible to increase the likelihood that others will change by creating a climate or culture that expects or requires it. The culture is affected by your behaviors and skills. Coaching is a management tool used to assist others in making behavior changes or skills improvement. A good manager is a good coach, and good coaching improves the likelihood of positive change.

The Five-Step Model for Effective Coaching

Before beginning the coaching process, you and the team member must agree on the topic and set the ground rules: when you will meet, how long you will meet, confidentiality rules, etc. Then the process begins. The five coaching steps and their components are listed below.

1. Set goals:　The coach assists the team member in establishing final performance objectives.

2. Discover lessons:　The goal of coaching is to get commitment to a higher level of performance. To do so, it is important that you help the team member to discover the lessons for himself or herself. Listen actively so that you can guide the team member to gain information and insight into the problem. Set things up so that the team member *sees the light*. It is probably helpful for you, the coach, to share your own experience. At the end of this step, the team member's short-term goals should be well defined and your expectations clear.

3. Explore steps: You and the team member must now decide on the steps required to achieve the short-term goals you have both agreed upon. Include action steps, suggest other references or people who might be helpful and support the decisions made.

4. Empower: At this point, review the key points you have covered to ensure agreement and understanding. Empower the team member to pursue the next steps and get agreement that these steps or expectations are acceptable. (Be sure that you have done your advance work so that as the member proceeds, he or she will not run into unnecessary stumbling blocks.) Lastly, and key to building a positive relationship and ongoing commitment, **express confidence** that the team member will reach the goals you have both set. Show enthusiasm for the team member's efforts. Encourage the team member to be more autonomous; foster her or his ability to achieve by conferring the power to achieve.

5. Review: To be certain that you have achieved the team member's commitment and understanding, at the end of the session, provide an opportunity for clarification. Ask the team member to review the coaching session and the goals and expectations you have both agreed to.

Counseling

This by no means suggests that you are expected to run a therapy session. Therapy of any sort is undoubtedly not in your job description. If you're wise, you will avoid helping someone to rid themselves of the neuroses and anxieties they have collected since birth. On the other hand, supportive counseling, as a management competency, is very much your job.

The following are some truths about counseling as a

management competency. Good counseling requires that you separate facts from feelings. In all counseling sessions, deal with feelings first (so you can get them out of the way) and then focus on facts and problem solving. To do this, and to counsel well, you will need to exchange information, which requires that you have skill in both questioning and answering. You will need to be sensitive to the individual and to the situation. Above all, you must show a sincere desire to listen, to hear and to understand all that is happening.

We will assume that, as a manager who has earned your stripes, you know the difference between open and closed questions and the relative value of each. You know that open questions reveal a lot of information and that closed questions elicit specific information and help direct the conversation. Remember that while closed questions are extremely useful, nobody likes to feel like they are getting the third degree, which often results from an endless stream of closed questions.

There is, however, an important questioning tool of which you may not be aware. It is the value of an "I" message. An "I" message requires that you speak, on occasion, from your own point of view. Instead of saying "you always..." or "why did you..." (both of which may sound accusatory to a vulnerable staff member), try expressing your perception from a personal point of view. You might say, for example, "what I think you're saying is..." or "I remember a similar issue I had when I..."

These "I" messages are little bits of self exposure. They are clear signals that you are listening in a non-judgmental way and that you care enough to share something of yourself.

Of course, you must not forget to clarify any mixed messages you may be receiving. You might say something like, "I'm not sure I follow, but..." or "maybe I'm out to lunch, but..."

Remember too that when the conversation bogs down, you do have some other tools at hand. Use reflecting or mirroring to get additional information and to lead the conversation forward. When you have heard it all, identify issues and diagnose problems. Help the team member to establish priorities and set specific goals. Then ask for solutions and, using positive language, help the member to create an action plan.

Summary

Exclusion is painful. A person who feels excluded cannot contribute their best because they feel that their efforts are undervalued or that nobody listens, or simply because their heart is not in it. Whatever the case, for superior performance from everyone on your team, inclusion is key. Include everyone, not just because it is the nice thing to do or even because it is the moral thing to do. **Include everyone because it is the smart thing to do.** Share decision making and impart your vision for peak results. Use your excellent communication skills to coach and counsel, and include each member of the team, because to get the job done well, everybody counts!

GETTING RESULTS

5

In Chapter 1, we explored the importance of relationships in the workplace. We revisited the subject in Chapters 2 and 3, albeit in a rather cursory manner. It is time to back up and take a brief historical glance at the workplace itself and how relationships have influenced results for the last several centuries.

In the earliest years of factories or plants, the owner of the operation was the boss, the chief in charge of everything. The owner/operator was a padrone, a man who looked after every aspect of his business, including the quality of the lives of the workers in his employ. He knew everyone by name, understood their strengths and weaknesses, and chatted with them daily, guiding them, encouraging them, directing their efforts and frequently "getting personal." He knew the names and situations of their wives and children and often acted as a sort of godfather to his employees and their families. If a worker's wife was ill, the padrone put his hand in his pocket and paid the bills. On special occasions, such as the wedding of an employee's daughter, the padrone provided a handsome monetary gift. It was customary for an employee to count on the padrone to come to his rescue in times of trouble or to share in the celebration in times of happiness.

The relationship between the padrone and the employee was not a contractual one. It was a sort of familial relationship and far more binding and mutually beneficial than a mere contractual obligation. In exchange for his voluntary largesse, for his paternalistic behavior and attitude, a padrone could count on his men to voluntarily go above and beyond the rigid confines of contractual duties. Indeed, employees (who often stayed a lifetime with one employer) could be counted on to do whatever was necessary to ensure that the padrone was financially successful; it was of mutual benefit to do so. Nobody checked the clock; everybody was invested in successful results. It was a fair trade: extra money for extra effort.

With the industrial revolution, the world saw the near demise of the padrone (which, in many ways, is certainly a positive step forward). Shareholders came into being. Owners were no longer on site and in charge of every aspect of production. Executives and administrators appeared. Overseers materialized. Managers were put into place. Supervisors were implanted. None of these workers in charge of other workers had either the permission or the funds to put a hand in his or her pocket for any reason other than to pay his or her own debts. As a result, the familial relationship of boss to employee disappeared, and contracts were devised with specific requirements. How else could the fair exchange of pay for work be ensured?

With the arrival of the employee contract, the moral imperative to go above and beyond, to take the extra step, vanished.

Of course, we can't go back. Nor would we wish to do so. Padrones had far too much power and influence than any working person would accept in today's hectic race for independence and individuality. Still, we must learn from the past and attempt, in some small way, to replicate the best in it, that "something" that produced results above and beyond. There once was something that used to result in achievement behaviors and we can try to recapture its essence. We can attempt to restore, in a modified, human way, the pivotal familial, warm relationship between manager and employee.

No matter how you measure success, results depend on the people who implement the plan. Since you, as a manager, are scored by the results of your people, you might be wise to ask yourself a few key questions if your goal is *getting results*.

For example, why is it that some people are given a task, dig right in and focus on achievement, while others do not? What is it that motivates achievement behaviors? Conversely, what are the barriers to achievement? Why can't I automatically count on everybody to do their doggone best every time? What can I do to motivate achievement behaviors and therefore produce exceptional results within the changing corporate environment? What are my relationships with my people and how do they influence results?

Maybe you need to examine exactly how you manage in order to manage at all. Let's face it, your job would be easier and your organization would benefit from employees who have:

- A strong commitment to the organizational objectives

- A superior ability to adapt to organizational change

- An exceptional willingness to perform

- A decreased need for counseling on performance issues

- Increased initiative in areas of accountability

- A willingness to share the vision

- A personal investment in building a culture of responsibility

In addition, real achievement brings benefits to your team members as well. Indeed, employees benefit because they:

- Break through personal obstacles to peak performance

- Take charge; achieve and maintain performance potential

- Establish action plans to achieve personal potential in key results areas

- Are more effective in their interactions on the job and in personal life

- Feel a sense of ownership, confidence and self-esteem

To think about achievement, one must consider empowerment as more than an aggravating addition to the new corporate lexicon. No one achieves if they are not convinced that they have the power, the capacity and the permission to do so. And something in the immediate environment must send the message that all of those pieces are in place. That something is, in this case, you!

Thus, you may need to develop your human relations skills and to sharpen your sensitivity by exploring the essence of positive interactions and the impact of your relationships on group dynamics. You must understand that the elements of human interaction are the cornerstone of the work environment and recognize your personal role as an agent of change. You need to develop alignment so that, together, you can pursue the vision.

Considering the strong motivating force of familial relationships, you might want to take the family analogy one step further. Think of yourself, the manager, as the head of your "family," not the outdated authoritarian model, but a good, progressive parent. A progressive parent is neither a dictator nor a padrone. A progressive parent provides the skills and support necessary to build strong and competent children, people who are capable of being successful on their own. Progressive parents lead their children forward by example and encouragement. They know when to interfere and when to back off. They prod, praise and provide essential guidance. Because of these characteristics, their kids grow into capable, successful and empowered individuals. And when they do, the progressive parent relates to them adult to adult.

As a premise and a process, the empowerment concept highlights the benefits of moving forward in pursuit of a cooperative working climate. It underscores individual accountability, accents valuing diversity and provides a solid base for skills application.

Then how do you achieve it? How do you provide the power, the capacity and the permission to achieve?

Recognizing the Importance of High Performance

For many organizations in the 1990s, the environment includes slow-growth or no-growth economies, global competition, decreased revenues, a need for innovation and productivity, and reorganization for positive advantage.

In fact, there is a very clear and growing demand for high performance. While adequate performance used to be good enough in the early days of the contract agreement, today's demands create pressures never before seen in the marketplace. Today, we demand employees who go well beyond the original job description. We want the sort of employees the padrone knew he could count on.

Current research indicates that business today needs employees who are self-motivated and innovative. We want action-oriented workers who are creative, confident and pragmatic self-starters. We expect to see a positive attitude. We want a problem solver who is decisive, resourceful and committed. Still, we need risk takers who can lead us into the next century. Is that asking too much?

In addition, researchers tell us we need team players who are participative, collaborative and cooperative. We want employees to focus on customer satisfaction, cost effectiveness, quality and productivity improvement. We demand flexibility, responsiveness, continuous learning and continuous improvement. Our workers want egalitarian work relationships, adult to adult.

We all recognize that the world is changing quickly and we must adapt if we are to be successful in a new and challenging climate. Current in-depth research indicates that the old "padrone" style of management is counter-productive to the goals of our employees today and to the culture an organization needs to be successful in a competitive climate.

To meet the ever-changing demands of the mercurial marketplace, you need a positive attitude and some realistic approaches to business and to managing others. If dictatorial paternalism and control do not work, you will need an alternative approach to be an effective manager.

Today's reality is that no company can foresee the future. Indeed, everyone is in transition, a state that will probably remain the only constant for the next two decades at least. The challenge is to be flexible enough and confident enough to manage your "family" within a constantly changing environment. No matter how good you are, you cannot do that alone. You depend on the skills, talents and motivation of the people who report to you. You need to stop directing traffic and start leading movement. Let's focus on the attitudes and behaviors a good leader champions so that the entire team is prepared and eager to build a culture that takes charge of tomorrow. Let's talk about relationships.

Who's in Charge?

If you think about it, your own manager is probably not present most of the time when you perform your job. Even when your manager is at the next desk or in the next office, that manager is not managing your job. You are; he or she is otherwise engaged.

Your manager may start you off by assigning a project or by giving you direction. Afterward, your manager probably reviews the results and may offer suggestions. This is a management function that requires only a small fraction of the time you need to get the job done.

In other words, in the actual execution of the work, you manage yourself. **You are in charge of you**. Conversely, you manage the individuals on your team for only a fraction of the time they are at work. Think about the implications of what that means!

In your organization, you have two functions: looking after others and looking after yourself. It is important to understand that you manage you. While you may have thought that, as head of the "family," you manage your employees all the time, from their point of view, this is not the case. They too manage themselves. They are in charge of their own performance.

Many important and insightful books have been written on the subject of transactional analysis, i.e., how people relate to each other. It is a rather simple model which says, essentially, that we have three possible ego states: parent, adult and child. The parent state dictates our rules of behavior, what we should and should not do. (When you hear that little voice in your head telling you not to drink so much at the company picnic, that's your parent talking.) The adult state is your rational side. It makes sense of incoming information and responds appropriately. (When somebody asks if you can help them with a report and you tell them you will, that's your adult talking.) The child state is the seat of our emotions—good and bad. (When somebody suggests you sneak out of the office for a quick game of golf and you feel a sense of excitement and just a little bit naughty and say, "Sure, let's go," that's your child talking.)

Often, conflicts arise which are difficult for the people involved to understand. Usually, one side has a sense that an underlying emotional button has been pushed, but cannot identify its source. Surprisingly, the other side may be totally unaware that anything at all is amiss. A simple analysis of the transaction may clarify the roots of the problem.

Psychologists tell us that it is crossed transactions that are the source of our communication problems. In other words, if you talk adult to child to a team member and that team member wants an adult-to-adult approach, you have created an unnecessarily uncomfortable situation for the team member. You may have unwittingly patronized, belittled, offended or simply pushed an emotional button. This is not a good thing to do when you want all your staff to take charge of themselves. You wouldn't expect a child to do a competent job, so you had better make sure you are engaging the adult in each of your members. It is the adult that gets the job done.

Your own adult is probably doing very well. After all, you achieved the title of manager; you must be pretty much in charge of your own success. Freedom to rely on our adult is critical to each of us, since how our adult manages our day-to-day activities determines how well we do in life. If you want employees to go beyond basic compliance and move into the realm of superior results, the quality of your relationships or interactions becomes key. The way you pursue your working relationships may need to be rethought.

First, it may mean that talking to employees as an autocratic parent would talk to a difficult child is a mistake. Your employees are, after all, in charge of themselves, just as you are. This means that now is the time to talk adult to adult. Your employees must be empowered to make many of their own decisions based on their own judgment. If every decision, every move, no matter how insignificant, requires your direction or approval, everyone's thinking adult will be shut down, and you will have nothing more than lackluster childlike performers waiting for their instructions.

Second, adults must receive the respect and consideration due them as decision makers, risk takers and perhaps even innovators. Naturally, as you are respectful of each individual, you are modeling the behavior for the rest of your team and redefining cultural expectations for all.

Finally, to energize and maximize the efforts of each worker for whom you are responsible, you will want to ensure a certain level of a caring, familial relationship. That is, you need to know your people as unique individuals, each with his or her own strengths, challenges and burdens. Understand that because they are all different, what motivates one may discourage another. Be aware that your own background, history or ethnicity may influence your perceptions and goals and that your priorities may not be shared by individuals of "different" backgrounds. Remember that communication is both verbal and non-verbal and that behaviors or gestures considered appropriate in one culture may be seen as quite the opposite in another.

Find out more about everyone on your team. Relate to them as people in whom you have a sincere interest, people about whom you care, and in turn, they will perform above and beyond mere contractual obligations.

Removing Barriers to Achievement

While historically the lessons of the padrone are intriguing, more recent research provides additional important data. A number of in-depth research projects exploring the attitudes and behaviors of high performers gives us an extra piece of salient information: achievement goes hand in hand with self-actualization. Maslow, in his studies of the hierarchy of needs, explains that self-actualization is the highest level of personal goal setting and achievement. It is reached only after all the other more basic needs, such as security, shelter and so forth, are met. Reaching that level of self-fulfillment occurs when or because an individual believes that she or he makes a difference. They understand that their personal contribution is of value. They know that they count. These deeply held beliefs result from the feeling that "I am in charge." Only a strong adult ego state is free to work from that paradigm.

It is up to you to remove the barriers to those achievement behaviors by supporting the adult state in all of your people. It is your responsibility to create a "comfort zone" for every employee. Free up the adults on your team so that each and every individual can do his or her best to achieve. You won't have to pay extra for it, but you do have to pay extra attention to get it.

Encouraging Achievement Through Influence

As with most organizational change, diversity initiatives provoke perceived negative consequences for some. Frequently, many employees routinely resist any sort of change. They may believe that it is unnecessary, that it is impossible to change a lifetime of learned behaviors, that some people will have an unfair advantage or even that their own jobs are at risk. Some may simply be so shaken by the mere suggestion of change that they are unable to think about it rationally and intuitively respond with a "no way" attitude.

In other words, you can expect some backlash to your call for change. You may discover that:

- People complain that they must divert time and resources from other programs to implement the desired change.

- Employees who have a vested interest in preserving the status quo actively oppose the initiative because they fear it threatens the security of their position.

- Because the benefits of the described change are not immediately obvious, nay-sayers attempt to demonstrate the folly of the initiative.

Whatever your team's fears or perceptions, a good manager is a strong leader. And strong leaders do not abdicate responsibility. Nor do they avoid influencing. In fact, to overcome resistance to diversity initiatives, you must be a positive influence; you will want to develop and apply both negotiating and managing conflict skills. Adult to adult.

The ability to influence others has been defined as a key capability for managers. You may want to focus on developing and enhancing your persuasion skills so that valuing diversity is truly endorsed by all employees.

Let's begin with an "influencing" quiz that measures your persuasion skills.

 Quiz

"Influencing" Quiz

1. During diversity meetings, you discuss your organization's mandates under the assumption that your employees understand the benefits.
   a. Frequently
   b. Occasionally
   c. Never

2. If your employees have an objection or they appear to resist, you begin by agreeing with them.
   a. Always
   b. Occasionally
   c. Never

3. When you talk with people, you use their names frequently.
   a. Always
   b. Occasionally
   c. Never

4. During discussions, you match people's pace, emotions and personal style.
   a. Always
   b. Occasionally
   c. Never

5. You illustrate points with anecdotes and metaphors as well as with facts.
   a. Always
   b. Occasionally
   c. Never

6. If employees are reluctant to speak up when they disagree with you, you draw them out by asking questions.
   a. Always
   b. Occasionally
   c. Never

7. You frequently say "we must" or "we have to" when discussing new initiatives.
   a. Always
   b. Occasionally
   c. Never

8. When people attack proposals or ideas, you retaliate by attacking too.
   a. Always
   b. Occasionally
   c. Never

Scoring

Give yourself 10 points for each correct answer.

1. c

   Talking about what's in it for each employee is the way to gain acceptance of your goals.

2. a

   Begin by agreeing or understanding the objection or reason for resistance. Then, work with the individual to solve the objection.

3. a

   Using a person's name creates rapport—but don't overdo it!

4. a

   Managers who adapt to others' communication styles make meetings and discussions more comfortable and productive.

5. a

   People are more receptive to suggestions when the point is sold with personal stories as well as with facts. (Self-exposure, adult to adult, creates positive responses.)

6. a

   You cannot effectively problem solve if people insist on avoiding the issue. Your use of good questions returns them to their comfort zone. Then, problem solving can begin.

7. a

Words like "must" and "have to" give a sense of urgency to your proposals.

8. c

You cannot effectively problem solve until people are in their comfort zones. Hear the person out and then begin to problem solve.

If you scored:

70–80:   You have superbly developed influencing skills and know how and when to apply them.

50–60:   You've got the basics. Work on some of the influencing techniques discussed in this chapter to increase your prowess.

40 or less: Work on developing your influencing skills. They will help you to increase your management effectiveness.

Affirming Progress

Diversity requires new organizational cultural practices, and employees must be encouraged to change their behaviors to adapt to these new practices. The role of the manager or leader is to model these new desired behaviors as well as to coach employees to display the behaviors. Coaching was reviewed in Chapter 4, but "growing" employees requires more. It demands that you use your influencing skills and negotiating strategies so that diversity programs are implemented without needless conflict.

Whenever we attempt to influence another person, we are negotiating. When negotiation occurs, it is clear that each person is out to win. Managers must use a win/win strategy when they are negotiating because a win/lose approach ensures a lack of cooperation and perhaps even sabotage by the loser. A win/win tactic guarantees that everyone is satisfied with the outcome and will work to make it succeed. It is your opportunity to affirm the progress you have made and to create a climate in which everyone is willing to work together in the future.

Successful negotiation requires planning. Begin by thinking through your diversity objectives for your organization. For each objective, answer the following three questions:

1. What do I want?

2. What do I need?

3. What is my timing?

Next, identify the potential resistance that will thwart your success. Some of the obstacles may be such issues as the impact of new working relationships, time limitations, past policies and procedures, or short-term (and long-term) disadvantages. Determine strategies to overcome resistance to the issues you have identified. You may want to consult with your colleagues and with your organization's diversity specialists. Learn from previous mistakes and plan ahead wisely. As Mark Twain said, "experience comes from bad judgment."

Because a win/win outcome is your goal, compromise is not a consideration. Indeed, compromise is an overrated problem-solving approach intrinsically designed to provoke all the players to focus on what they have lost or given up. Compromise may be the solution of last resort in a stalemate situation, but this is a situation in which everybody wins if you play your cards right. For each of your diversity objectives, you must decide what benefits will accrue to everyone involved when your objectives are met. This is not a simple step, but it is a necessary one for developing alignment. Focus on the positives: what they get, when they get it, why they get it, how much they get and what you expect in return.

Equally important to planning the negotiation is the negotiating process. To make diversity programs work, a supportive, cooperative environment is required. To ensure you are building a positive climate, always begin the process by stating your diversity objective, accompanied by a positive statement such as, "I am committed to making sure this initiate works in a way that benefits everyone." Then wait for feedback. Now is the time to listen to and understand any concerns employees may have. Because you have thought this through in advance and anticipated most of the issues, you will have solid benefit statements at the ready to counter each objection.

Your game plan is designed to resolve each issue with win/win strategies, to align all the players and to ensure that all eyes are focused on the same goal. Seasoned negotiators recommend that you begin with a minor issue that can be easily settled so that a supportive, problem-solving climate is established. You can use this early success to affirm progress.

Still, some issues will be controversial and difficult to resolve. However, because you have planned for each issue, you know what you want and what you need. Present what you want, but not what you will settle for. To get what you want, keep focused on positives at all times.

Of course you must work with employees to discover what they want too. Because this phase of the process can be stressful for everyone, it is important to remember that resolving differences is not a test of power. Win/win solutions are essential to your diversity success. Gambits such as "how would you feel if," "maybe we could" or "what about" are often helpful in influencing the conversation and swaying the outcome. It is during this negotiating process that everyone will focus on the benefits of change if you have structured the discussion well. The trick is for you to maintain your focus on the benefits your team will get; in doing so, you get what you want.

When the issue is settled, be sure both you and the employees understand the agreement. Point out the progress you have made together and be sure to write the decision down at the end of the meeting to eliminate any and all possible misunderstandings after the fact.

Diversity initiatives, like any other major change effort, may cause intergroup conflict, which must also be managed. Conflict does indeed have many negative consequences such as lost productivity, reduced morale or decreased motivation. However, avoiding conflict is no solution. The problem rarely goes away by itself. Like any family quarrel not confronted, unresolved issues tend to fester and take on unnecessarily major proportions. Since some resistance and conflict is almost certain, your role is to diagnose the cause of conflict and to resolve the issues so that organizational effectiveness is strengthened and the hostility to change is eliminated.

A variety of strategies can be used to manage conflict. The appropriate strategy depends on how critical the issues are to accomplishing your organizational goals and how skilled you are at using the strategies.

Managing Conflict

Avoidance is a perfectly acceptable option when the issue is unimportant. There are certainly instances when ignoring conflict is the best solution because it simply does not matter. However, you should be aware that trivial issues can sometimes be symptoms of a larger, more significant issue that you might want to explore.

When the issue is important, use your influencing

skills and *negotiate* for a successful solution. The negotiating process is a valuable management tool for resolving conflict and requires that employees work together to
agree upon mutually satisfactory solutions. Take your
time and think the issue through. A short-cut is often the
longest distance between two points! Choose to negotiate
when there are many possible solutions and you want the
group to make a decision because you believe that, given
the benefits of a positive outcome, you can count on a
win/win result. Negotiating encourages constructive con-
frontation and group involvement, which result in high-
quality solutions to diversity issues.

When you expect that the issue will create a win/lose
scenario and that group consensus is doubtful, you may
wisely choose to *mandate*. If, in your judgment, a decision must be made that is unlikely to be acceptable to all
employees, mandating may be the only way to go. Be
aware, however, that imposing a solution rarely ends the
conflict—it usually just disappears for a while or shows
up in disguise. Bulldozing also tends to incite a "digging
in" mentality.

The following Positive Change Model demonstrates
the steps in the process required to make successful
change. If the change you have called for has bogged
down before new habits and behavioral patterns are established, you may have missed one of the key steps.

Positive Change Model

Call for Action

- point out benefits
- develop alignment   ↓

Practice Positive Behavior

- reinforce positively

New Habits/New Patterns

 **Worksheet**

Planning for Accomplishment

Diversity objective:

1. What do I want?

2. What do I need?

3. What is my timing?

Potential resistance:

a.

b.

c.

d.

Benefits that are likely to overcome resistance:

a.

b.

c.

d.

Win/win strategies:

- What do they get?
- When do they get it?
- How much do they get?
- What do I expect in return?

Motivating Alignment

The following are some simple suggestions to help you achieve your goal.

1. Use inclusive language in all your written and oral communications.

2. Make a formal presentation to all the stakeholders. Present a strong business case and point out the benefits of your diversity initiative.

3. Invite a panel of "diverse individuals" to share an open dialogue with your staff. Have them address the issues they have had to confront in the workplace.

4. Invite a legal specialist for a "lunch and learn" session. Address the consequences of inequity or harassment in the workplace.

5. Contact a local community care association and invite a speaker who is "physically challenged" and can speak to your team about a variety of barriers to equal opportunity.

6. In some public and positive way, recognize the "early adopters," those individuals who are helping you to champion the change.

7. Create a community outreach program to help you get to know your customer better.

8. Avoid the phrase "affirmative action" because it is often inflammatory and therefore counter-productive.

9. Set up a continuous learning team whose mandate is to educate about diversity issues in whatever way they choose.

10. Ask for suggestions to move your diversity initiatives forward.

 **Story**

The Farmer and the Scarecrow

Farmer John stood at the edge of his newly sewn corn fields and felt his anger rising. As he surveyed the deep, rich furrows, great black birds began to gather on the ground and peck greedily at the tasty corn seeds beneath the brown, corduroy surface.

"Not this season," Farmer John thought, as he waved his rake and shouted angrily. "I've not arisen at dawn, day after tiring day, and worked my fingers raw to feed a bunch of miserable freeloaders."

Farmer John had a plan. Assembling all the pieces—fresh hay from the barn, a frighteningly bright red shirt, newly laundered overalls, fireman's boots and a big straw hat—he began to construct a perfectly awesome scarecrow. When it was finished, he carried it out to the middle of the corn field and tethered its back tightly to a long wooden pole he stuck conscientiously into the earth. Next, he stuck a broom through one sleeve and fed it across the back of the scarecrow through the other sleeve, thus lifting the long arms menacingly. As he worked, the birds stayed clear and Farmer John was pleased.

"Now listen," he said to the scarecrow. "This is my land, but you are in charge. It is your job to keep those beastly birds away. Frighten them off any way you can think of. You are the new master of my corn fields. You have the power here. I grant you total freedom to achieve the goal I have set for you." And off he strode, confident that great change was now well underway.

The scarecrow was delighted, of course. Being new at the job, he thought painstakingly about the best strategy to adopt, should the fearless birds appear once again. As he thought, the hungry birds began to assemble on the ploughed furrows. Soon, there were masses of birds ravenously plucking seed from the newly planted earth.

The scarecrow tried to wave his arms, but they were fixed to the pole. He labored vigorously to wiggle his straw fingers, but he wasn't exactly sure how that might be done. He struggled gamely to shake his awesome head, but it was tethered too tightly to the pole. He wanted to kick out with his big black boots, but he had no idea where to begin to do such a thing.

"Fly off" the scarecrow wanted to shout, but he didn't know how.

Soon, Farmer John returned, enraged at the scarecrow's complete failure to do what he had so clearly been charged to do.

"What's the matter with you?" he roared. "I gave you the perfect job for a scarecrow. I handed you absolute authority and unlimited power to do anything you wanted in these fields. What more could you possibly want?"

"I just don't know," thought the disappointed scarecrow.

Lesson

No one is empowered when they are tied down.

Questions

1. How does this lesson apply to our organization?

2. What can I change now that I know what I know?

3. What other lessons does this fable hold for me?

Summary

Getting results depends on creating an environment in which you engage the adult in each of your employees through respectful, empowering relationships. It means helping your team to overcome barriers to high performance by modeling a caring attitude and redefining behavioral expectations. Getting results requires your leadership, sensitivity, influence and motivational skills.

FAIR MEETING GUIDELINES

Every manager holds meetings. Every good manager holds good meetings. There sure are lots of good reasons to hold those meetings, according to the managers who call them. Remember that a meeting needs a reason, and it usually must be more than simply providing information, which many on your team may perceive as a waste of their valuable time. Provide necessary information before the meeting, and use the meeting to:

- Discuss

- Review progress

- Problem solve

- Sell an idea

- Train

- Motivate

- Provide opportunity for sharing and input

Many managers consider meetings a good time to demonstrate their authority or to wield their power, but meetings should be more than that. They can be a perfect opportunity to build an equitable culture, so make your meetings fair.

Good meeting involve five steps.

Prepare

Before calling any meeting, you must **identify the goal of the meeting** and prepare yourself well enough that you are confident that goal will be achieved. Preparation also means creating an agenda with prioritized items. Anticipate problems that might arise and develop strategies ahead of time that equip you to confront those problems successfully.

Publish the Agenda

In communicating with your team about the upcoming meeting, you will, of course, need to tell them the time, the place and the duration. You must also let them know what is on the agenda and inform them of the goal of the meeting. Hopefully, you will be clever enough to do this in the form of a benefit statement, so that everyone you are inviting will have the answer to the universal but unspoken question, "what's in it for me?"

When you send out your notice, ask for additions or comments to consider before the meeting, so that those participants who may be otherwise reticent are given an opportunity to speak up or to add an item they feel is important. Advance publication provides direction for the meeting and tends to keep everyone on track and focused when they arrive.

Structure

The most important structural rules of a good meeting are:

1. Start on time

2. End on time

3. Lead in the middle

Let's assume that as a good manager, you always achieve Rules 1 and 2. Our focus here is on managing Rule 3. Well in advance of the meeting date, consider your agenda items and prioritize them. Weigh each item and allow sufficient time for the most important items to be dealt with thoroughly; allot minimal time for unimportant items. If you have too many items on the agenda, eliminate those that are least urgent. You will never get to them anyway, and there is nothing to be gained in making everyone feel that they have failed.

Decide which items require consensus before you will be able to move on and which items can be settled by a vote or an individual decision. The points that need agreement may take a little longer than you anticipate, so allow some extra time. Place the less important items, or the ones that can be easily and quickly addressed, at the end of the meeting. You may not get to the last one, so be aware and be prepared.

In structuring your meeting, remember that diversity in your workers includes differences in thinking styles. Consider these differences when you are figuring out your time requirements, because if this is a problem-solving session, you will need to include everyone.

Manage the Process

When you open the meeting, be sure to set the ground rules. Remind everybody about the goal of the meeting and ask for full participation. Then, *listen, level and lead.* Listen to what is being said. Hear what is not being said, i.e., what is carefully and obviously being avoided. Listen to the words as well as the non-verbal communication. Listen to whomever is not contributing and manage to involve them. Expect everyone to contribute.

Leveling means offering your observations and being honest about what you think you see. If the meeting is going well, compliment everybody on the progress the team is making. If the meeting gets off track or things are going badly, say so in an open, self-disclosing "I" statement such as, "It seems to me we've already covered that" or "I'm not sure you heard what Julio said before." You could also say, "I think we're beating this thing to death" or perhaps, "Listen folks, we need agreement on this. And fast." You may want to restate the process you have agreed on by saying, "Nancy, we decided we would reach consensus on this one and nobody would try to bulldoze their idea though." If you notice that one of your participants is unfairly on the attack or being deliberately unkind or vicious, interrupt with a leveling comment and restate the ground rules. If a member is locked into his or her prejudice, a meeting may not be the appropriate time to tackle the problem because a bigot will not reason and a fool cannot reason. As we all know, a little ignorance goes a long way, so if, in your judgment, the issue needs immediate attention, confront the disturber with a clear statement like, "Prem, that's not acceptable around here."

Lead the meeting forward. Use visual tricks such as checking off completed agenda items to indicate that progress is being made. Use humor freely, but never demean a member of your team or yourself. Never crack a joke at another's expense; nobody ever forgets where you buried the hatchet! Sidetrack *disturbers* and keep all participants focused. Even if, as a way of sharing the power, you have passed the meeting over to another team member, as a participant it is always constructive to do your part to keep everyone on track. When you believe you have reached consensus, you might move on by asking, "Is everyone okay with that?" or "Does anyone disagree?"

Leading also means being up front about admitting your errors. Managers, like computers, often make very fast mistakes. If you have missed something, say so. If you do not understand a point being made, ask for clarification. Sometimes, when the team has gone off in an unexpected but valuable direction, it is best to be silent; a closed mouth gathers no foot.

One of the key reasons for holding a meeting is to stimulate discussion. After all, if you did not want discussion, you could have sent a memo. Remember, your role here is not to dictate results, but to guide participants towards the outcome you want. A good way to stimulate discussion from the outset is to start with warm-up exercises, several of which are described in Chapter 7. Of course, you can also stimulate discussion by directly asking for input. "Jan, what do you think about what Mario just said?" "Sal, tell us more." Ask the group for their ideas, their thoughts and their comments. Provide paper and pens for written comments, to be collected or noted on a flip chart. (Sometimes it is easier for some people to write things down.) Keep the discussion on the topic. Engage the silent members by moving closer towards them or by asking them directly. Turn away from dominating members of the group. Use a P.I.N. chart (see Chapter 7) and require each participant to contribute five thoughts to each section. Try brainstorming or brainwriting (both can be found in Chapter 7) to free up creativity and to improve participation.

If the meeting you have called is a long one and people start to get "that glazed look," call a break, focus on a different activity or introduce a brain-teaser (see Chapter 7) to liven things up again. To really shift the mood, you might want to read the story of "The Fire in the Forest" (Chapter 7). When everyone is refreshed and rejuvenated, go directly back to your agenda.

Five minutes before the meeting closes, remind everyone that time is nearly up. Summarize what you have achieved; state what still needs to be done. Thank everyone for being so helpful.

Record

To ensure shared understanding, record all decisions, action steps and tangible results. You do not need someone to take minutes; just send around a post-meeting recap to all participants. And remember your manners; say thank you for coming.

Dealing with Disturbers

Disturbers, whatever their tactics, can be divided into two types: those who want to dominate the discussion and those who want to sabotage it. In either case, you must have a few maneuvers ready to derail disturbers.

If you have identified a potential disturber before the meeting even begins, try a preemptive strike. Speak to the person and enlist his or her support ahead of the meeting. It might be a smart tactic to designate a task or role to the person and perhaps even to tell them why. Alternatively, you might ask others to ignore the disturber ahead of time. Another option is to schedule an item on the agenda for dealing with disturbers, and transfer responsibility for dealing with that person to the team.

If someone does succeed in derailing your meeting, you may:

- Stare at them until they are embarrassed enough to stop

- Ignore them

- Say something directly, like "that kind of thing isn't acceptable around here"

- Use body language to express your displeasure

- Intervene and ask another member to speak

- Ask the group to deal with the disturbing behavior

Keep your temper and your dignity; a loose piece of flak tends to find the nearest eye. Remember to encourage a win/win solution and don't belittle anyone in your attempt to get the meeting back on track.

Diversity Topics

In pursuit of your diversity goals, it is a good idea, at every meeting, to include one agenda item that specifically addresses diversity issues. Use the agenda item to stimulate discussion and action. Let the team take it from topic to deed by asking something open, like "What shall we do about this?'"

Some agenda item suggestions are:

- Creating a diversity team
- Creating a support team
- Planning a diversity day
- Dealing with inequity
- Accessibility—what do we mean?
- Building an equal opportunity environment
- Exploring differences
- Improving our communication
- Learning about each other
- Using our talents
- Building respect
- Recognizing differences as benefits to the team

Another good idea is to share responsibility for setting the agenda. After all, whose meeting is it anyway? Then again, you may simply choose to open your meeting, or close it, with one of the helpful bits or pieces from

Chapter 7. Improve your meetings every time by keeping your own notes on a "Last Meeting Worksheet."

Summary

Fair meetings result from careful planning, preempting dysfunction and sharing of responsibilities.

 **Worksheet**

Last Meeting Worksheet

Goal:

Agenda:

Who attended?

Did everybody understand the purpose?

Did everyone participate?

Who did not?

Strategies to involve non-participant next time.

What worked well:

What did not work well:

TEAM-BUILDING EXERCISES

7

*The path to creativity begins
with the suspension of judgment.*

Creating a link with your co-workers develops a positive attitude toward change and promotes good feelings of working together toward excellence. Creativity often plays an important role.

A strong team is an effective team. In a strong team, members support each other, decisions are superior, people are productive and the quality of the work is improved. People are happy to go the extra mile because they care, about each other and about not letting their team members down.

Every time you open the conversation and invite the team to participate, you are building the team. Every time you ask the team to problem solve, to set new goals, review processes or even to play together, you are strengthening the bonds between members.

The following is a collection of team-building exercises. Some of them are "Quick Hits" and can be used in part or in whole as meeting openers, coffee-break teasers or the basis for communication sessions or problem-solving sessions. Other exercises may be used as workshop events. You can choose to use them in any combination that makes sense to you and your organization.

Jeopardy

Instructions

Use the following list of answers. Either divide the group into two competing teams or have individuals supply the questions. Score one point for every good question. Score two points for every thought-provoking question.

You can use the entire list or use only one question to open each session.

There are no right or wrong questions. The goal is to get people thinking and talking, to heighten awareness and responsibility.

Process

The answer is: *communication*
The question is:

The answer is: *empowerment*
The question is:

The answer is: *discrimination*
The question is:

The answer is: *opportunity*
The question is:

The answer is: *education*
The question is:

The answer is: *ignorance*
The question is:

The answer is: *the unknown*
The question is:

The answer is: *prejudice*
The question is:

The answer is: *exclusion*
The question is:

The answer is: *teamwork*
The question is:

The answer is: *politically correct*
The question is:

The answer is: *sensitivity*
The question is:

The answer is: *fairness*
The question is:

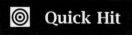

Who's Your Type?

1. Tell your team that this is a simple self-test with no possibility of failure.

2. Tell them that the test is absolutely unscientific because we are not using a control sample of thousands, but it is a great way to start understanding differences.

3. Use the test as a conversation opener, a keyhole view of the mix of your team or simply as a message to let your people know that you are interested in them.

Goals

1. To improve self-awareness

2. To demonstrate that diversity issues include differences in style

3. To develop awareness that the personal style of others must be considered

Process

A. You often feel exhausted.
B. You can run two miles easily without feeling tired.
C. Running is for gazelles.

A. You are often pressured by lack of time.
B. Time is a resource you use to your advantage.
C. Time is irrelevant.

A. You frequently "double up" and do two things at once.
B. You do one thing at a time.
C. You put things off until later.

A. It is important to make a good impression.
B. You generally make a good impression and don't worry about it.
C. What other people think doesn't matter at all.

A. To get things done right, do them yourself.
B. Delegate the job if you can.
C. Everything will get done in its own good time.

A. If you could improve your organization, you could increase your productivity.
B. You are as efficient as anyone needs to be.
C. Productivity is for rabbits.

A. You often feel physically tense.
B. You find relaxation easy.
C. You love to sleep a lot.

A. You have set long-term goals and are concerned that you may never reach them.
B. You have set some life goals and feel confident about reaching them.
C. Goals are for hockey players.

A. You find stupidity irritating beyond belief.
B. You find stupidity interesting.
C. Who's stupid?

A. You play to win.
B. Winning is fun.
C. Winning is nice.

A. You dislike being reminded of what you need to do.
B. You accept reminders as helpful.
C. Reminders keep you on track.

A. You are sometimes aware of a sense of urgency.
B. You are not upset when you postpone a deadline.
C. You dislike time constraints.

A. You walk quickly.
B. You walk at an easy pace.
C. You stroll.

A. You are a stickler for details.
B. Details clutter your mind.
C. Details are for obsessives.

A. You often wake up early, thinking of all the things that need doing.
B. You sleep very well.
C. You love to sleep.

A. You feel that you have outstanding leadership qualities.
B. You accept a leadership role when necessary.
C. You are relieved not to be in a leadership situation.

Total: A _____   B _____   C _____

Scoring

Count up the A's, B's and C's. Whichever is greatest would be your "primary style."

Results

1. A's tend to be perfectionists. They are often driven to succeed and focus on details and outcomes. They are often highly successful and push themselves beyond their own comfort level.

2. B's tend to be flexible and easygoing. They can focus when necessary but don't appear to have an internal need to push themselves beyond what is comfortable. They tend to be content and easy to get along with (except for A's, who might find them too careless).

3. C's tend to be so relaxed and undemanding of themselves that it is unlikely they will hold down a regular job.

It Could Be a Wonderful World

If we could consider each other
A neighbor a friend or a brother
It could be a wonderful, wonderful world.
It could be a wonderful world.

This little ditty has been sung by young children for generations. The thought is a lovely one, but we know that ours is not a perfect world.

This exercise might help us to begin some problem solving in our work world.

From This Moment On

1. In a perfect world, if someone around here insulted someone else (intentionally or not), one of us would

   _____

   _____

   From this moment on in our world, if someone around here insults someone else, we will_____

   _____

2. In a perfect world, a newcomer to our organization could expect_____

   _____

   From this moment on in our world, a newcomer to our organization can expect _____

   _____

3. In a perfect world, if one of us told a dirty joke at work, another would_____

    _____

    From this moment on in our world, if one of us tells a dirty joke _____

    _____

4. In a perfect world, if one of us is being excluded from the rest of us, we would _____

    _____

    From this moment on in our world, if one of us is being excluded from the rest of us, we will_____

    _____

5. In a perfect world, if one of us belittles or demeans a particular minority group, another would_____

    _____

    From this moment on in our world, if one of us belittles or demeans a particular minority group, another will _____

    _____

6. In a perfect world, if one of us has special needs, another would _____

    _____

    From this moment on in our world, if one of us has special needs, another will_____

    _____

7. In a perfect world, if one of us insists on being dis-
    criminatory, another would _____

    _____

    From this moment on in our world, if one of us
    insists on being discriminatory, another will_____

    _____

8. In a perfect world, if one of us poked fun at someone's
    lifestyle, another would. _____

    _____

    From this moment on in our world, if one of us
    pokes fun at someone's lifestyle, another will_____

    _____

9. In a perfect world, if one of us brought prejudice into
    the workplace, another would _____

    _____

    From this moment on in our world, if one of us
    brings prejudice into the workplace, another will

    _____

    _____

10. In a perfect world, if we noticed bias and barriers
    that interfered with success of some, another would

    _____

    _____

    From this moment on in our world, if we notice bias
    and barriers that interfere with success of some,
    another will _____

    _____

Stepping on Toes

If someone steps on your toe, accidentally or otherwise, it may be painful for a moment or two but you usually recover in a matter of minutes. However, if the poor toe under siege happens to be sore or sensitive, or if the klutz who caused the injury just happens to be slightly bigger than a Buick, you may suffer from your wound for a long, long time.

Let's ponder what might be considered stepping on toes.

It's Stepping on Toes When:

1. _____

2. _____

3. _____

4. _____

5. _____

6. _____

7. _____

etc.

 **Workshop**

Stranded

Goals

1. To establish common values

2. To explore the concept of stereotypes

3. To provide an opportunity for team building

4. To have fun

Process

You and your team have been abandoned in the Sahara. You have no idea how far you are from civilization or from help. Checking with each other, you discover that among you, you have:

1 camel

1 gallon of fresh water

2 half-full water flasks

2 chocolate bars

1 nylon tent

1 knife

10 gold coins

1 sleeping bag

1 Bic lighter

the desert clothes you are wearing

1 compass

A passing caravan refuses to let you join them, but offers the following choices:

- A bag of gold coins in exchange for your camel

- One of their camels for one of your teammates

- One of their camels for three items of equal value

The caravan plans to leave at daybreak. Decide what you will do.

Debrief

1. What did you learn from this exercise?

2. Did your group work as a team? If not, why not?

3. What does this exercise tell you about values?

4. How did you handle conflict?

5. How do some of the lessons from this exercise apply to our work goals?

Quick Hit

Team Spirit

Everyone wants to know:

- How am I doing?

- What are the goals?

- What can I do to improve?

Motivating the team:

Ask your team to list ten ways to tell them "you are doing fine."

1. _____

2. _____

3. _____

4. _____

5. _____

6. _____

7. _____

8. _____

9. _____

10. _____

 **Quick Hit**

Performance Award

Everyone needs to hear something good about themselves. Everyone wants recognition and a sense of feeling valued as a team member. You can provide that opportunity for your team by using a performance award. Even though this award is presented by way of a structured exercise, it has a wonderfully positive impact on participants.

Invite everyone to sit in a circle and hand out the awards. Ask each member to create an award for the person on their right. When they have done so, ask that they pass the award to the person to whom it was written. Give each person a few moments to digest their award and provide an opportunity for conversation.

Process

I enjoy you because:

You are terrific at:

What I respect about you is:

And in addition:

 **Quick Hit**

Winner of the World Championship

Your company's reputation for creativity and innovation in design and development is so widespread that it is generally believed your skills would be applicable in a variety of areas. Therefore, your team has been asked, by the International Symposium on Excellence in Supermarket Marketing and Delivery Systems, to submit a creative design for a new and improved grocery cart.

This is an international competition, and the prize will be presented to the winning team at the United Nations in New York.

Design the Cart:

Debrief

1. Provide an opportunity for each design to be presented and appreciated.

2. Discuss the benefits of working creatively together.

What Bugs Me

Even if we don't understand the sensitivities or "sore spots" in another individual, we have an obligation to respect them. In this exercise, everyone gets to write down what "bugs" them, which provides an opportunity for ventilation, discussion or action.

Viewpoint Exercise

Your local zoo has been the proud home of the rare and endangered Chickenkiller Eagle. Yesterday, the prized eagle escaped, sending shock waves around the office and the rest of the civilized world.

Write a newspaper report on the eagle's escape from the point of view of:

1. The eagle

2. The zookeeper

3. An animal rights group

4. The local chicken farmers

5. The local politicians

Debrief

1. Discuss the impact of "position" on point of view.

2. Discuss the strategies for reaching consensus among people with differing viewpoints.

3. Discuss the value of having fun together.

Workshop

Time Capsule

You have been selected to choose three items for a time capsule to represent the 1990s and to be opened in the year 3000. You have been given no restrictions and no parameters; you are free to choose as you wish. Choose carefully.

_____

_____

_____

After everyone has written down their selections, discuss them. Look below the surface for commonalities. Use the information to kick off serious discussion about what is important to everyone and as a way to learn more about each other.

Debrief

1. What have you learned about yourself?

2. What have you learned about each other?

3. How could we take all of the items you listed and reduce them to a final three items for the capsule—and achieve consensus?

To Reward Successes

When your team has achieved success, it is important to reward them. Provide colored pens, crayons, paper and a variety of cutting and pasting equipment for a fun activity with team-building value. Use the banner they create to hang on the wall for everyone to see or give to the "Champion of the Month."

Ask your team to design a "Champion Motto."

Brainwriting

1. Think about your goals for improving the climate and getting the best from the diversity of employees on your team. Write a "wish statement" about the team.

2. Pass the written wish clockwise and ask each team member to suggest a solution and pass the paper on to the next person.

3. Each group member adds a suggested solution to the list.

4. When the list returns to you, discuss all the solutions provided.

5. Invite your group to take action, and ask where they would like to begin.

I wish:

Brainwriting solutions:

How Is It for You?

For this exercise, ask your team members to write their answers privately (low risk) so you can gather them up and discuss the ideas with the group.

Then say, "Imagine that we work in a perfect organization. It is spectacular! It is sensational! In fact, it is almost miraculous. What happens around here that makes it so?"

A Personal Vision

Most organizations have a vision statement written on the wall. It helps them focus on what is really important. A personal vision statement does the same, but it can be used to do more. Use it to learn more about your people and to provide an opportunity for each of them to learn more about each other.

Objectives

1. To get in touch with core personal objectives

2. To explore how your vision impacts your contribution to our team

3. To provide an opportunity to examine what success means to you and where you are on the path to goal achievement

4. To provide the energy for peak performance

Process

Symbols are useful for sending messages, but also for helping to identify core values. For example, everyone knows that a red cross stands for relief of human suffering and a red maple leaf symbolizes Canada.

Since each of us is different, this activity will help you to discover and clarify what is really most important to you—your goals and values—and your potential for achieving them. Because each of us is similar in some ways, this activity will also help us to discover and clarify what values and goals we have in common.

Begin this exercise by thinking deeply and looking inward for a few moments. Ask yourself about your most important goals. You may have thought often about things like starting a fitness program or getting enough money to travel more often. But think deeper. Think about the inner you, who you are and what you expect in life.

This experience will help you to discover some of the secrets you may be keeping, even from you.

Instructions

Answer the following questions:

1. What would I like my epitaph to say?

2. What has been a deep learning experience in my life?

3. What characteristics or traits do I want to improve?

4. What characteristics or traits do I like best about me?

5. What am I best at?

6. What do I want to accomplish in my life?

7. What do I need to enrich my life?

8. What are my most important possessions? Why?

9. Who am I?

10. What person, living or dead, would I most want to be like?

Keeping your answers in mind, create a symbol for each of the following: work, family, leisure and friends. Choose symbols that represent your dreams and goals, to create a symbolic picture of the real you.

Your vision:

Workshop

An Equity Vision

Even if you do not choose to have every one of your staff create a personal vision, writing a department or team equity vision is a valuable exercise for a variety of reasons. It immediately sends a very clear message that you take the concept of valuing diversity very seriously. It offers an opportunity for every voice to be heard. Once completed, it not only creates a department mandate, it articulates a behavioral requirement.

Gather your team and work on the vision statement together. Begin with something like, "In this department, we recognize..."

Consider including the following words in your vision statement; they will also help the group focus on the goal of the exercise: value, merit, significance, worth, dignity, importance, benefit, appreciate, esteem, regard, treasure, difference, distinction, harmony, respect, consider, consideration, cooperation, equal, equitable, even, equivalent, contribute, augment, reinforce, strengthen, participate, take part, welcome, unity, wholeness, solidarity, fellowship, accord, share, common, believe, deem, expect, envision, demand, require, accountable, responsible, answerable.

Affinity Table/Affinity Wall

The affinity table is a problem-solving tool that often is used to allow a problem to solve itself. It is used when you have more issues, ideas or opinions than you believe you can handle easily or when you suspect that open discussion may lead to more conflict than is productive.

The table is more a creative than a logical process, but, surprisingly, it is a remarkably reliable tool.

1. With your team, brainstorm the diversity issues you wish to consider.

2. Generate and record ideas on index cards or Post-Its. (No criticism of ideas is permitted. All ideas are recorded.)

3. Put the index cards on the table (or Post-Its on the wall).

4. No talking is allowed. Everyone is involved in moving the index cards or Post-Its into related groups that make sense to them. If you don't like where a card is, move it to a better spot.

5. This process does not have a time limit. At some point, all movement of cards and Post-Its will cease. At that point, create header cards to capture the central idea of each group of cards.

6. You now have groups of issues with some specific action steps. Use these groups as problem-solving strategies.

 **Tool**

Warm-Up Exercises

1. Without lifting your pencil from the paper, use four straight lines to connect the dots below.

    o   o   o

    o   o   o

    o   o   o

2. Plant four trees so that the root balls are equidistant from each other.

3. You have ten trees. Make five rows of four trees each.

4. What five-letter word do you find in the following letters?

    H   I   J   K   L   M   N   O

5. Which is heavier, a mountain or a mistake?

6. Which is more thought provoking, a window or a door?

The Design Idiom

Creating a P.I.N. Chart*

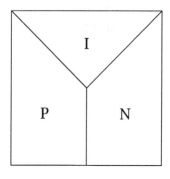

Conflict is almost always (there are never absolutes) based on a clash of perceptions or on each side working from a different reality base than the other. When one side states what it believes to be a good idea, the usual result is a clash of ideas, goals and attitudes.

Our usual method of dealing with the other side's good ideas is to argue or to negotiate, both of which are attempts to use logic or power to get what we want. Either way, one side states the thesis, and the other side states the antithesis; the goal is to destroy the other's possibility of winning. Different perceptions lead to different goals. But what if we could change perceptions without attacking the other side just to prove them wrong, stupid or vicious?

There is a better way. The **design idiom** is based on a mutual agreement to explore ideas and therefore approaches problem solving constructively, moving the matter forward rather than arguing events or perceptions of the past.

The **P.I.N. chart** provides a structure for exploration. P is for positive; all the positive results of implementing the idea are noted here. I is for interesting; all the interesting but not necessarily relevant results of implementing the idea are noted here. N is for negative; all the

* Based on ideas described by Edward de Bono in his book, *Conflicts—A Better Way to Resolve Them* (Penguin Books).

negative results of implementing the idea are noted here. The P.I.N. chart invites a new way of thinking.

Now create the setting. Because the P.I.N. chart focuses on breaking down patterns and perceptions (i.e., thinking in a new way), every technique that encourages creative or lateral thinking should be brought to bear. This means stimulating as many of the five senses as you can in an effort to avoid vertical thinking. For example, instead of writing notes on paper, use a large horizontal board or flip chart or craft paper on a wall. Use colored markers. Play pleasant background music if you like. Distribute crayons or colored pencils and colored paper for private doodling. Work in a room with a view. Scatter simple toys about, such as slinkys and nerf balls. Provide a creative setting. Then:

1. Draw your chart.

2. Using the colors of your choice, print a big "P" in the lower left section, a big "I" in the upper section and a big "N" in the right section.

3. Invite everyone to focus on the Positive section. Ideas should come from both sides to fill in the section. When it appears that everyone has run dry, switch focus to the Negative section, and invite comments from both sides. If discussion here triggers another thought to add to the Positive side, or vice versa, do so.

4. Ask everyone to focus on the Interesting section, and explore the interesting outcomes that might arise. These are thoughts without value judgment.

5. Discuss and explore.

There are many ways to use the P.I.N. chart, including:

1. To help your team explore and evaluate ideas and to stimulate new insights. In the process, they may discover that they have changed their mind.

2. When two sides are in opposition.

3. To "triangulate" the exploration. Use a third person as a design catalyst to provoke creative thinking. This person is neither a go-between nor a judge. This person is charged with asking intriguing questions that stimulate creativity.

The Fire in the Forest

Inexplicably, one late spring afternoon, a terrible fire raged through the little green forest beyond the pasturelands, past the trout creek and over the rolling hill beyond. Wrathful flames ravaged the trees and devoured the tiny plants that flourished on the rich, dark forest floor. The furious fire filled the rabbit holes with soot and leveled the nearby beaver's house as angry fingers of flame reached out to consume it whole. The cruel blaze destroyed the careful anthills and vaporized homey birds' nests. By nighttime, the fire was gone, and with it, most of the animals that had called the little green forest their home.

When a cool breeze blew across the ravaged wood and it was clear that the fire had truly retreated, the survivors poked their frightened heads out into the starry night and looked tentatively around. Slowly, they gathered together at the base of a charred old oak and began to take stock. Almost nothing remained as they knew it; home would never be the same again.

Brown Bear, deep in his forest cave, had survived the dreadful assault rather well. He had smelled the bitter singe of hardwood in his nostrils and had heard the terrifying crack of blaze and awesome din of disaster, but Bear himself, was barely touched. Being the biggest brute among the creatures of the forest, he decided to take charge.

"Listen," he said to them. "If you do as I say, you will all have new homes by morning. And they will be bigger and better than the cramped little quarters you lost."

The animals, being nearly as afraid of Bear as they were of the terrible inferno, sat and waited quietly for instructions from their new leader.

"Rabbit," said Bear turning to Greyback Rabbit, "dig your new borough here," as he indicated a charred breach between two great rocks. "You will be safe next time a fire invades because the sturdy rocks will always protect you."

"But Bear," suggested Rabbit, "those big grey boulders are only part of the great grey rock beneath. I cannot possibly dig a proper home there."

"Nonsense," said Bear. "I know the forest as well as you, and I know what is best." So Rabbit began to dig.

"Robin," said Bear, "build your new nest here," as he indicated a sooty, burned out place beneath two fallen timbers. "You will be safe next time a fire invades because those charred trees will not burn again and they will always protect you."

"But Bear," said Robin, "my family must live in a tree."

"Nonsense," said Bear. "I know the forest as well as you, and I know what is best." So Robin began to build.

"Beaver," said Bear, "build your new dam here," as he indicated a watery puddle at the foot of a hilly crest. "You will be safe next time a fire invades because this puddle trickles down from the high hills. It is far enough from the undergrowth that flames cannot reach it, so the puddle will always protect you."

"But Bear," said Beaver, "I need a bubbling brook to build a good two-story family dam."

"Nonsense," said Bear. "I know the forest as well as you, and I know what is best." So Beaver began to build.

By morning, all the animals had surveyed their work and decided their efforts had been in vain. Again they gathered together at the base of the charred old oak and began to mutter amongst themselves.

"I can't even dig a proper hole in those rocks," lamented Rabbit, "never mind a wonderful warren with winding rooms and comfy birthing quarters. That meager dent will never be a proper rabbit home."

Then Robin spoke up. "I can't build a proper nest on the ground." she moaned. "My precious eggs will be trampled by those careless deer before the tender babies are even hatched. And how will I teach my dear fledglings to fly with no branch as a launchpad?"

"I quit," said Beaver. "I can't build a two-story dam in a puddle! Where will I put the recreation center? Where is the trap for the fish supposed to go? A puddle is simply no place for a proper beaver family and a proper beaver dam, damn it!"

Sitting nearby, Bear overheard the disgruntled mutterings and was stunned by the haughty disobedience of the weak little forest creatures he had being trying to help. Bear pulled himself up on his great hind legs and bellowed, "Nonsense. I am a great and powerful big brown bear. I am stronger and craftier than all of you. I know as much about caves as you do, Rabbit. I know as much about trees as you do, Robin. I know as much about water as you do, Beaver. I know the forest as well as any of you, and I know what is best."

"Perhaps you know what is best for you," whispered the animals.

Story Questions

1. What does this story mean to you?

2. Do we see any of Bear's behaviors around here?

3. What are the possible outcomes of those behaviors?

4. How else might the animals have handled their problem?

5. What other ways might Bear have helped the animals?

6. Were the results predictable? If so, why? If not, why not?

7. What does this story have to do with diversity issues?

Big Upset in Marcus Mouse Brawl

Minutes after the swing-shift change, a brawl erupted in the parking lot at Anywhere Industries. Anywhere is well known as a champion of diversity in the work force and claims to be an equal opportunity employer.

Marcus, acknowledged by his own legal counsel to be the aggressor in the fight, was charged with aggravated assault and filed a counter harassment suit against his supervisor, T. Tiger. Tiger had severely aggravated the mouse by allegedly calling him a big-eared rat just before the shift change.

The lawyer for the supervisor advised the press that he plans a "humor" defense on behalf of his client. The supervisor will claim that Marcus is just *overly sensitive*, and the comment was made all in good fun. "The little fellow should just mellow out," the supervisor said in his own defense.

Lawyers representing both sides appeared at the bail hearing. Management claimed innocence and refused comment.

This is not the first time that Anywhere Industries has been the site of unmanaged diversity. Thea Wont, administrative assistant at AI for 17 years, last month was granted an undisclosed settlement when the jury agreed that the humor she had endured for years was no joke.

Management has asked you to help tackle the diversity issue for the beleaguered company.

Story Questions

1. What does this story mean to you?

2. Do we see any of the supervisor's behaviors around here?

3. What are the possible outcomes of those behaviors?

4. How else might Marcus and T. Tiger have handled their problem?

5. Were the results predictable? If so, why? If not, why not?

6. What does this story have to do with diversity issues?

Story

"Managing Me" Awards

Every employee, from top to bottom, at the Talent Unlimited plant in downtown Urbanville received a Managing Me award from the company president in a moving ceremony at corporate headquarters last night.

Cleaner Will Lowman was asked by this reporter how he had earned the award. "Since my manager is so busy, I'm the one who actually manages me. I am in charge of my own performance. I manage me and I must say, I do it rather well. I think I deserved the award."

In a speech from the podium, company president Bob Bigman agreed. Said he, "We are more efficient and more productive than ever before. It's great news and something to celebrate. Everyone here is tops."

Story Questions

1. What does this story mean to you?

2. Do we see recognition for self-management success around here?

3. What are the possible outcomes if we don't?

4. How can we celebrate the good work we do ourselves and we see others do?

5. What does this story have to do with diversity issues?

 Focus Group

Focus Group Guide

Focus groups are routinely used to begin the process of information gathering or to check on progress in a variety of situations. Clearly, the value of focus groups is that they can provide a great deal of information when there is a need to know.

It is important to note that your corporate culture will be replicated within the focus group room, so it is crucial that you pay close attention to both what is said and what is avoided. That means that any problems existing within your corporate culture will likely reveal themselves in the focus group setting. Put another way, if minorities feel oppressed within your organization, they are likely to feel oppressed within the focus group—and you will not hear from them. Remember too that the direction and outcome of the focus group will depend on you, the leader, within the context of the organizational culture.

In selecting your focus group, make sure that all of the participants in each group are at the same level in the organization so that communication is as free and open as possible. Don't trust everything people say; some will tell you what they think you want to hear and others may worry about the politics of speaking out or the problems of differentiating themselves from the group. Use the information you gather only as an indicator of what is really happening. Be sensitive to wounds and be prepared to deal with serious problems appropriately if any are identified. (For example, you cannot ignore a complaint of sexual harassment if it is revealed to you.)

Process

Introduce the purpose of the focus group with something like, "We are here to explore our diversity program." Then use the following questions as your focus group guide.

1. What diversity initiatives are currently in place in our organization? (If people do not know, be prepared to tell them.)

2. How does our diversity program affect you? How does it affect others in our organization?

3. What are the fears? The expectations? The rewards?

4. How are we doing? Are we making progress?

5. Where are we falling down on the job?

6. How could we do better?

7. What are the signs of trouble? Of success?

8. What are we forgetting?

9. What can I do to help?

10. What should happen next?

Story

Backward and Forward

According to time-honored custom, everyone in the town of Klutz was required by law to walk backward, and the practice appeared to work quite well for the thoughtful inhabitants of the charming old town.

"No better way to know where we've come from!" they told each other cheerfully in town meetings.

"An effective tradition for honoring our illustrious past," they agreed in assemblies.

"A clever practice for faithfully remembering our distinguished roots," they allowed aloud.

Now, it was also true that the town had more than its share of garden-variety accidents, but everyone agreed it was important to go along to get along. A misstepping citizen might easily slide down the crusty banks of the little river that meandered quaintly near the edge of the town, but rarely did anyone venture so far from home. A careless shoe might unhappily discover a painful pothole newly grown overnight, but generally, the town took fierce pride in anticipating disaster and tolerated no great risk; careful attention was paid to every pebble on every road at every possible opportunity. So, all in all, a little backwards thinking put everything into the right perspective and the townsfolk managed remarkably well—until someone changed the law.

Nobody knew who changed it because it's hard to look back to the back of your back. Nobody knew who changed it because most people are blind behind their behind. Nobody knew who changed it because it's impossible to face what your face does not face. But the law was changed nonetheless. No one could walk backward from that moment forward. And the whole town was suddenly beside itself.

"What will we do if we have to walk forward?" they asked incredulously at town meetings.

"How will we get ahead if we must always look ahead?" they queried fearfully at assemblies.

"How can we look forward and backward at the very same time?" they wondered aloud.

As was their custom, for seven days and seven nights, the town's wise generals met to discuss the challenge. Perhaps the change should be undertaken gradually. Possibly the transition should be a slow one. A conscientious person might begin by walking two steps forward and two steps backward.

Or maybe people could learn to turn in careful little circles as they walked, thereby ensuring a 360-degree view at all times. Of course, everyone had a different learning curve in Klutz, even as they do everywhere else, and the slower learners might be whirling into town for a lot longer than some of the quicker citizens, creating an obviously unfair advantage for a fortunate few.

Still, the generals thought and discussed, counseled and visioned, and on the sixth night, they were blessed with a sudden and wonderful insight. If everyone undertook to abide by the law, and everyone initiated the change at the very same time, everyone could help anyone who needed help.

"I have a better idea still," said the clever town mayor. If we want to look forward and backward at the very same time, why don't we just look in a mirror?"

"Yes, but will it work?" asked the town.

Questions

1. What is the lesson in this story?

2. How does this lesson apply to our organization?

3. What can we change now that we know what we know?

4. What other lessons does this fable hold for you?

QUICK AND EASY PROGRESS SURVEY

 **Tool**

Let's see how we're doing. Use a scale from 1 to 10 (1 = poor; 10 = excellent) to help you assess your progress. Your answers will be subjective, of course, but this tool will give you a clear picture of your perception of where you are now and what specific areas you identify as still needing work. It will help you to focus and maintain your own motivation. Update your answers every three months and keep track of your progress.

1. Does *everyone* understand that diversity gives us a competitive business edge?

2. Does *everyone* understand why I am promoting our diversity initiative?

3. Does *everyone* make a serious effort to include?

4. Have we eliminated exclusive or offensive comments and behaviors?

5. Is *everyone* sensitive to diversity issues?

6. Does *everyone* take personal responsibility for creating a "better" culture?

7. Is *everyone* comfortable here?

8. Do I have a system in place that promotes real, multi-directional communication?

9. Is *everyone* going the extra mile to produce superior results?

10. Do I *always* counsel when necessary?

11. Do I *always* coach when necessary?

12. Do I *always* provide equal opportunity?

13. Do I *always* provide personal growth and skill development opportunities when I identify a need or when an individual requests it?

14. Have I succeeded in transferring responsibility for continuous learning?

15. Do we have sufficient support structures in place?

16. Do we provide "sharing" opportunities?

17. Are our relationships *always* respectful?

18. Does *everyone* appear to feel empowered?

19. Does *everyone* get help when they need it, without my intervention?

20. Has turnover decreased?

21. Are we a synergistic team? (Do we always access our own expertise and use it to the best advantage?)

22. Does *everyone* contribute what they can?

23. Is *everyone* focused on achievement?

24. Do we celebrate success?

25. Do we celebrate each other?

26. Do I hold everyone accountable for managing themselves?

27. Have I provided the environment and the tools for self-management?

28. Is this a *trusting* environment?

29. Do I handle disturbers appropriately?

30. Do I model the behaviors I want to see in others?

WHERE DO WE GO FROM HERE?

9

Columbus Lost En Route

Following a recent re-engineering of the global map, Christopher Columbus set out to rediscover the New World. En route he was astounded to find the Atlantic Ocean had been moved.

CEO I.M. Queen of the WOW (What a World) Organization explained, "Massive reorganization, right-sizing and an in-depth analysis of the current global marketplace indicated a major shift in paradigms was in order. Accordingly, moving the ocean and thereby eliminating the influential Atlantic currents made perfect sense. We could see that we needed to outreach, network and isolate at the same time, a conundrum indeed. But, with the diversion of the Gulf Stream, we were assured a more direct route into the world economy."

Unprepared for the subtle undercurrents of this audacious move, Columbus was confounded in his attempts to cross the sea. The Nina, the Pinta and the Santa Maria were last seen foundering in a whirlpool at the base of Niagara Falls, now located in upstate Wales. Columbus himself was saved by the Bell, a recently refurbished and rechristened Maid of the Mist.

Medics on the scene reported that the disheveled Columbus was heard to mutter, "Who knew?" on his way to seek personal assistance.

The manager reading this piece of alarming news offered invaluable expertise in helping Columbus to chart a new course when he is ready to venture out again.

So Where Do We Go?

You have decided to chart your new course. You have caucused, discussed, planned and presented. You have empowered, communicated, coached and counseled. What do you do next?

The following is a collection of ideas to help you plan your moves. Post them. Place them on worksheets. Use them as committee mandates. Find an application that works best for you and your team.

Bright Idea

1. Create a diversity resource center. Stock it with books, videos and pamphlets from a variety of community organizations and help groups.

2. Build a "diversity" music library and ask people to bring in "ethnic" music to be loaned out.

3. Select a process for ethnic celebrations or heritage days.

4. Invite speakers.

5. Create a newsletter that highlights the benefits of diversity and celebrates differences.

6. Celebrate every holiday you can find, in a short, symbolic way.

7. Create an ethnic recipe book. Ask for grandma's best recipes.

8. Post a calendar of events that includes anything and everything applicable.

9. Invite your staff to your home or out for a casual, social get-together.

10. Have a lunch-time sing-along. Ask everyone to write down the lyrics to a simple "old country" melody and teach it to the rest of the group.

 **Worksheet**

Use following worksheet to help you keep track of all the good things you have set in place.

Project: Start date:

Who is in charge?

Who is involved?

What is the mandate?

What are the short-term goals?

What are the long-term goals?

Another step that will plant everyone's feet firmly in the right direction is to ask everyone on your team to fill out an action plan specifically focused on their personal role as an agent of change.

◄ Action Plan

As my personal contribution to our valuing diversity initiative, I plan to:

1. _____

_____

2. _____

_____

3. _____

_____

My short-term goal is to_____

_____

My first step is to _____

_____

My long-term goal is to_____

_____

The benefits to others that I identify as a result of my efforts are _____

_____

The benefits to myself that I identify as a result of my efforts are _____

_____

*Signed*_____

INDEX